In Drought Time

Scenes From Rural and Small Town Life

A Collection of Poetry and Art

In Drought Time
Scenes From Rural and Small Town Life

A Collection of Poetry and Art

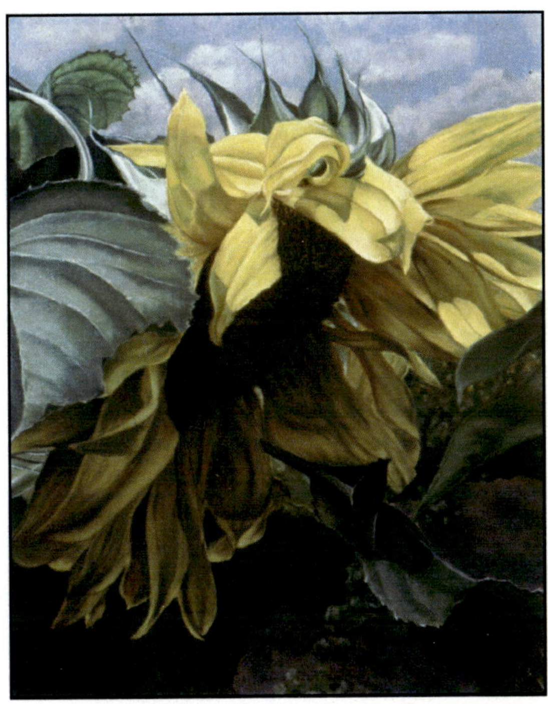

Backlit Sunflowers, *MaryBeth Koeze*

Edited by Douglas M. Smith, Melody Vassoff, and Karen Woollams

Mayapple Press 2005

Published by   Mayapple Press
               408 N. Lincoln St.
               Bay City, MI 48708
               www.mayapplepress.com

ISBN 0-932412-37-8

ACKNOWLEDGMENTS:

Laura Kasischke's poem, Local Legend, first appeared in *Housekeeping In A Dream*, Carnegie Mellon Univ Press, 1995. Blizzard at the Chelsea Fair, first appeared in *Gardening in the Dark*, Ausable Press, 2004.

Judith Kerman's poem, Microeconomics, first appeared in *Seeding the Snow*.

Thomas Lynch's poem, Vigil, first appeared in *Still Life In Milford*, W. W. Norton & Company, 1998.

Richard Tillinghast's poem, What We Bring to the River, What the River Brings to Us, first appeared in *Huron River: Voices From the Watershed*, University of Michigan Press, edited by John Knott and Keith Taylor, 2000.

Elaine Wilson would like to thank Nick And Elena Delbanco, Fred Horowitz, Celeste Adams, Sadashi Inuzuka, and Chris Donnelly.

The Editors of *In Drought Time* would like to thank Kathy Klem, Jean Lau, William Brody, Ellen and Phil Pochay, Marijo Grogan, Kent Ashton Walton, Manuela Heaney, Nancy Paul, Debra Vassoff, Cecily Donnelly, Geoffrey and Rose Smith-Woollams, and the Chelsea Painters for helping in their own unique ways to make our book possible.

Book design and typesetting by Karen Woollams. Cover in Bradley Hand and Lucida Sans; section titles in ITC Bradley Hand; text in Lucida Sans.

Cover design by Karen Woollams and Judith Kerman.

Cover photo, It's Been A Bad Year, Stan Woollams.

Table of Contents

Country

From Winesburg, Ohio—*Sherwood Anderson*
Long Shadows Go Out From the Bales—*Elaine Wilson* ... 3

French Notes—*MaryBeth Koeze* ... 4

Funky Landscape—*Nancy Feldkamp* ... 6

A House in the Country—*Doug Smith* ... 7

Sentinel—*Susan e. Pulju*
Winter Crow—*Joan Painter Jones* ... 9

The Dairy Farm—*Marijo Grogan* ... 10

Cows in the Barnyard—*Mildred Dowling Clark* ... 12

Tornado, April 3, 1956—*Elizabeth J. Westrate* ... 12

Great Blue Heron—*Susan e. Pulju*
Patience—*Stan Woollams* ... 13

October 20—*Jay Stielstra*
Untitled—*Laura Strowe* ... 14

Roadkill—*Brad Tomkins*
Black Birds—*Nancy Feldkamp* ... 15

Silos at Solstice—*Elaine Wilson* ... 17

What We Bring to the River, What the River Brings to Us—*Richard Tillinghast* ... 18

Spring River—*Ruth Gilmore Langs* ... 19

Three Women—*Meaghan Powell* ... 20

Nightime Trip to Migrant Camp on Esch Road, Manchester—*Carol Rose Kahn* ... 21

Autumn—*Jay Stielstra* ... 22

Golden Days—*Jean Lau* ... 23

A Pilgrim's Progress—*Marijo Grogan* ... 24

Pa, Sonny and Horse—*Mildred Dowling Clark* ... 25

Once—*Richard Tillinghast* ... 26

Meadow—*Jacqueline Hoats Shields* ... 27

Hoarfrost on Lima Center Road—*Elaine Wilson* ... 29

Untitled—*Laura Strowe* ... 30

Map—*Elizabeth J. Westrate* ... 31

Landscape, 1963: The Rock—*Keith Taylor*   32
Up the Hill—*Jacqueline Hoats Shields*

Untitled—*Melody Vassoff*   33
Flower Girl—*Madeleine Vallier*

Vigil—*Thomas Lynch*   34
Moonstruck—*Ilona Brustad*

Untitled—*Melody Vassoff*   35
White Carnations In a Blue Vase—*Alyce Frank*

Sandra, Meet the Moon—*Sandra Xenakis*   36

Untitled—*Laura Strowe*   37

Ayers' Barn Raising—*Mildred Dowling Clark*   39

The Moment—*Oscar Marx*   40
Eaton Road—*William Brody*

Death of the Hired Tractor—*Brad Tomkins*   41
Breuninger's Silos—*Elaine Wilson*

Missionaries on the Porch—*Doug Smith*   42

Haying Season—*Teresa Freed*   43

Rapeseed Field—*Teresa Freed*   44

The Rapture—*Marijo Grogan*   45

Hungering for an Answer—*Rosemary Caruso*   46

Fallen Icon—*Jean Lau*   47

Tracks 2—*Alexandra Tinsley*   49

Spring Thaw—*Teresa Freed*   50

Sunday's Song—*Doug Smith*   51

Thirty Pounds—*Hermione Miles Gorney*   52

Grandma Fuller's Chicken—*Mildred Dowling Clark*   53

Mast Road, Misty Morning—*Elaine Wilson*   54

Waiting for Silence on North Territorial Road—*Kent Ashton Walton*   55

Farmer—*David B. Sing*   56
Pa in the Corn—*Mildred Dowling Clark*

Town

From Winesburg, Ohio—*Sherwood Anderson*   57
Common Grill—*Greg Sobran*

Words—*Ilona Brustad*   59

Hall M—*William Brody*   60

This Town—*Elizabeth J. Westrate*   61

Subliminal Industrial Dreams—*Gregory Parker*   62

Two Vents and Water Tower—*Russ Marshall*   63

Blizzard at the Chelsea Fair—*Laura Kasischke*   64

Untitled—*Katherine Larson*   65

Old Time Diner—*Elizabeth J. Westrate*   66

Diner—*William Brody*   67

11 Sighs at Zou Zou's Café—*Doug Smith*   68

Chelsea 4—*Greg Sobran*   69

Village Without a River—*Doug Smith*   70
Big H—*Elaine Wilson*

Steeple Tower—*William Brody*   73

Backlit Sunflowers—*MaryBeth Koeze*   75

From My Father's Garden—*Catherine Croisant Varner*   76

Untitled—*Laura Strowe*   77

Bellwether—*David B. Sing*   78
CC Dowling—*Mildred Dowling Clark*

Microeconomics—*Judith Kerman*   79
October Sky—*Sandy Knapp*

Clothes on the Line—*Hermione Miles Gorney*   80

Untitled—*Laura Strowe*   81

Chain-link Fence—*Kent Ashton Walton*   82
Fence Boy—*Joan Painter Jones*

Contradiction—*Oscar Marx*   83
Loaves and Fishes—*Heidi Kraepel*

Footgrab—*Alexandra Tinsley*   85

Untitled #1—*Melody Vassoff*   86
Roses on a Table—*Alyce Frank*

Burn—*Melody Vassoff*   87
Salmon River—*Heidi Kraepel*

Untitled #2—*Melody Vassoff*   88
Early Morning—*Madeleine Vallier*

Spring—*Melody Vassoff*   89
Dreamlike Shell of the Past—*Monette Thorrez*

Peach—*Hermione Miles Gorney*   90
Ripening—*MaryBeth Koeze*

Sunburst—*Stan Woollams*   91

Chairs—*Jacqueline Hoats Shields*   92

Out of the Garden—*Rosemary Caruso*   93

Eggs and Toast—*Gregory Parker*   94
Still Life with Coffeepot—*James Peery*

Stained Glass—*Gregory Parker*   95
Red Tree—*Teresa Freed*

Local Legend—*Laura Kasischke*   96

Whispered Secrets—*Monette Thorrez*   97

Drought—*Hermione Miles Gorney*   98
Into the Light—*Ruth Gilmore Langs*

There Are No Poems Here—*David B. Sing*   99
Lesley's—*William Brody*

Contributors

Poets   100
Artists   101

Poetry is knowledge, salvation, power, abandonment. An operation capable of
changing the world, poetic activity is revolutionary by nature; a spiritual exercise,
it is a means of interior liberation. Poetry reveals this world; it creates another.
Bread of the chosen; accursed food. It isolates; it unites. Invitation to the journey;
return to the homeland. Inspiration, respiration, muscular exercise. Prayer to
the void, dialogue with absence: tedium, anguish, and despair nourish it. Prayer,
litany, epiphany, presence. Exorcism, conjuration, magic. Sublimation, compen-
sation, condensation of the unconscious. Historic expression of races, nations,
classes. It denies history: at its core all objective conflicts are resolved and man at
last acquires consciousness of being something more than a transient.

Octavio Paz

Country

In the fields are planted berries and small fruits. In the late afternoon in the hot summers when the road and the fields are covered with dust, a smoky haze lies over the great flat basin of land. To look across it is like looking out across the sea.

Sherwood Anderson from Winesburg, Ohio

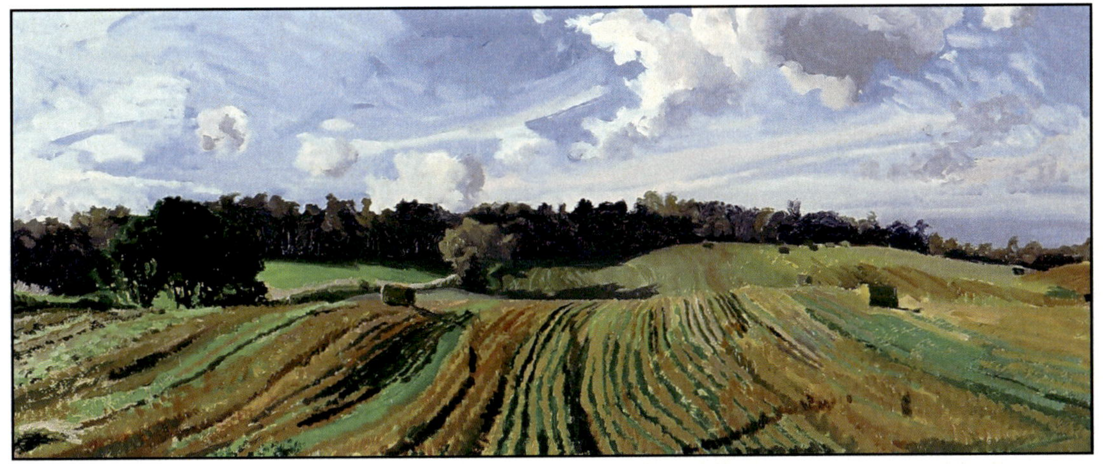

Long Shadows Go Out from the Bales, *Elaine Wilson*

...miracles don't come free...

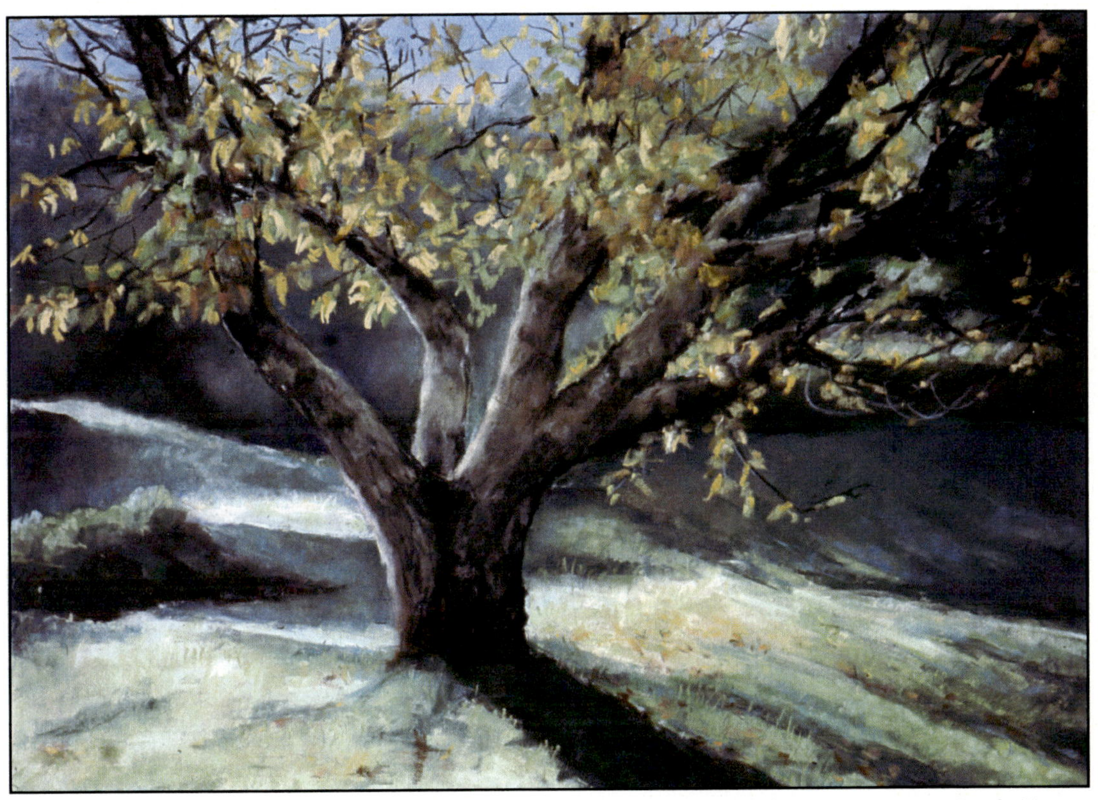

French Notes, *MaryBeth Koeze*

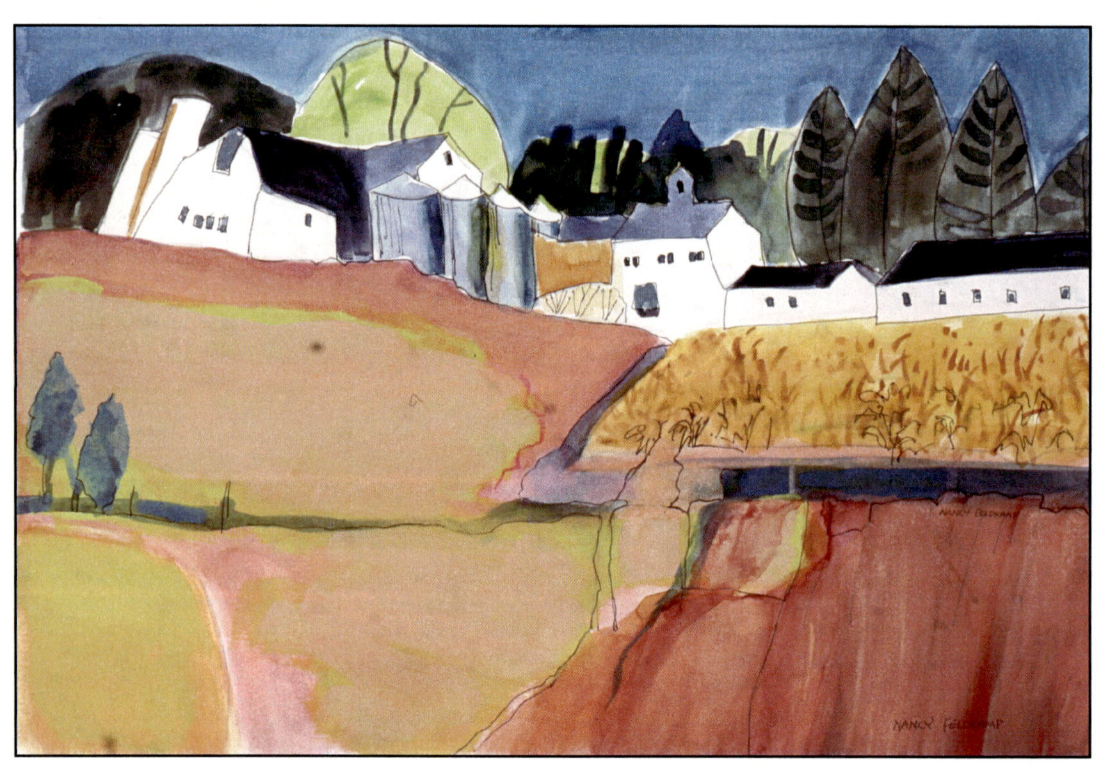

Funky Landscape, *Nancy Feldkamp*

A House In The Country

He moved to the country
with his wife and children
sixteen hundred feet off a dirt road
in a gray two story house
on a gentle slope
between a marsh and a corn field.
There are trees but not too many.
Down the hill, a pond crawling
with frogs and muskrats, but no fish.
Neighbors urge him to dig out the pond
and stock the brown water
with blue gill and bass.
He's quit talking to his neighbors.
He plants trees.

Along the front of the house
his wife tends a garden,
studies, plans and waits years
for the lilacs and day lilies, roses
and spirea, iris and dogwood
to grow and bloom into one
great botanical documentary.
She doesn't grow vegetables,
they buy vegetables in town.

In the summer, he walks
the fields behind his house.
Son, daughter and dogs
tramp alongside. He takes
snapshots of the young feed corn
asleep and maturing
in lime green husks,
photos of the roots, stalks
jutting out of the ground
looking like mangled ghoulish
yellow fingers desperate to grab life;
pictures of his unripe heirs
stumbling over uneven ground,
banging into cornstalks,
tripping over pregnant roots,
feigning mortal wounds
among thorny weeds,
disappearing into the tall slender
lush green curtains.

He loves the walks, the feel of
moist dirt under his heels
and cool dry air
pushing through the countryside,
pushing through him.
At night, lying in bed next to his wife
the interstate hums in the distance
as an orchestra of crickets join the
jack hammer pounding in his heart.
He hears his children's laughter, the
dogs' frantic barks, all chasing a doe
into the brambles flushing two sand
hill cranes hidden among the rushes,
cattail, and wild raspberry bushes.
He sees his young heroes tackle
the dogs saving the cranes from
being bitten as they labor to lift off
screeching like flying dinosaurs.
Exhausted, his daughter staggers up
the well-worn path, hands him five
clam shells found near the creek.
    How beautiful they are.
"You found them here?" he asks.
"So many colors, it's a miracle, daddy."
Restless, he rolls over on his side,
away from his wife, faces the doorway
leading to his children's bedroom.
His eyes close, daughter's face lingers
in the air, five shells wet in his palms.

Doug Smith

The Sentinel

On a high slight limb, the crow faces another day

She calls
To the east
To the sun that brings forth light

On our fractured land

Light that deepens
Rows of corn fields
Rows of soybeans
Roads that cross other roads bloating in squares to the horizon

Spreading night wings
She lifts into the certain
Morning, an ash waving
She calls

Circling over streams of cars
Their custodians rushing to their concrete
Dominion moving over the face
                    of the world moving away

She calls

She calls.

Susan e. Pulju

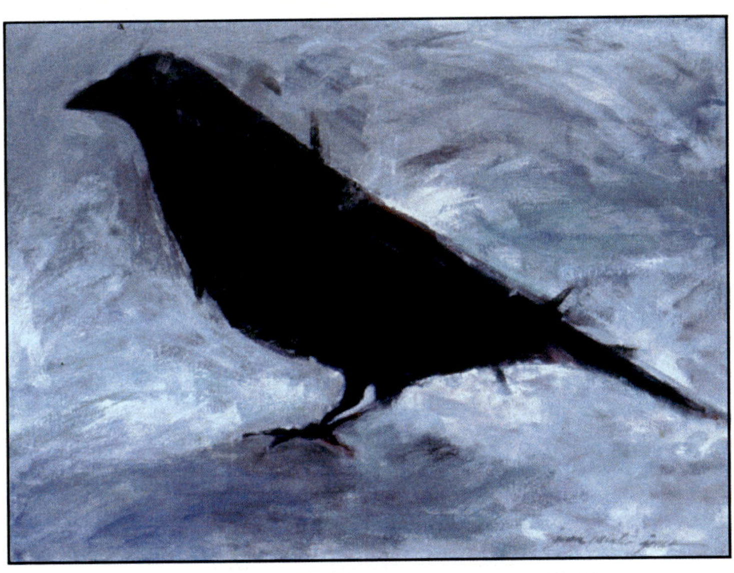

Winter Crow, *Joan Painter Jones*

The Dairy Farm
(Dedicated to Lloyd and Arlene Grau)

Outside the village runs a dirt road.
At the end of this road lies a dairy farm.
And on this farm a man prepares to sell his herd—
an act marking the end of an era
stretching from the dawn of time
when human and beast shared the land together.

Every morning for 45 years
he has risen to be with them,
these gentle beasts with large eyes
"his girls," he calls them.
In the barn with bowed head
he receives their greeting,
a blessing so like that of grandmothers,
the purveyors of old tales,
guardians of birth and death.

In the kitchen on a winter's morning,
the farmer's wife will no longer look for
the clotted clouds of their steaming breath
rising from the yard where the garden grew.

And on summer afternoons,
she'll no longer spy her husband in their midst
a tight intimate group in the hollow of a hill
exchanging gossip over clover and purslaine.
She'll no longer see these matrons in their
black housedresses spotted white
like the sprawling clouds passing overhead.

"The new dairy," her neighbor proclaims,
"looks neat and efficient," painted red and white
like a Ramada Inn, a huge hospital or university.
Inside thousands of cows stand on cement slabs
their teats connected to the iron lung
of a milking machine, producing without end,
milk we will spill across our counters
or down the drain when prices fall.

And in among the lot will be the farmer's girls
waiting for the touch of his hand on their heads,
waiting for the barn door to swing open on the morning.

Marijo Grogan

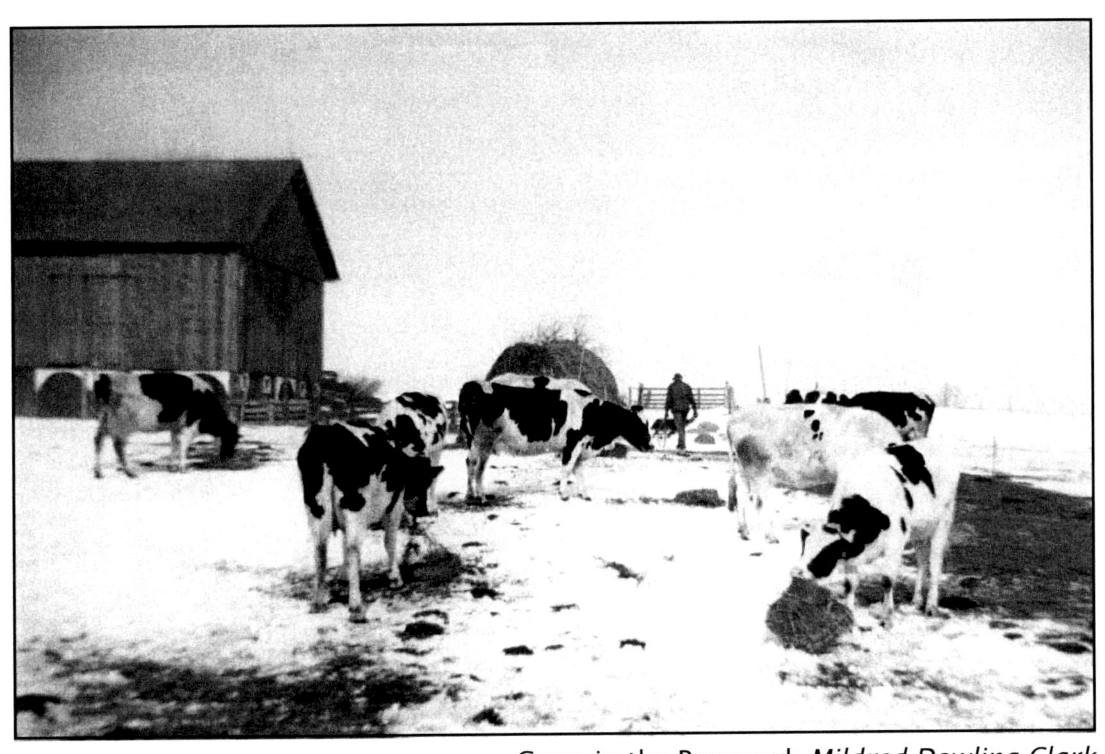

Cows in the Barnyard, *Mildred Dowling Clark*

Tornado, April 3, 1956.

Storm, high wind, a shift of rain
hung loose at the shoulders
with skipping stone clouds:
and their dash-dash-dash-v
dash-dash-dash-v patterns.

A mother's classic study of storm
at the front picture window
she followed the lightening fingers
mapped, scanned the shape of clouds
in the dim, located the funnel cloud
then rescued two children
five year old son, two year old daughter
they ran, carried, held hands
down stairs to the basement
followed by the sound of:
       rushing trains, freight trains
       ten pairs of railroad tracks, five engines
       a thousand coal cars with baseball bats.
       taking turns, breaking glass

they held hands, carried, ran
from shooting straws, sticks
through hollow tubes, blow darts
that aimed for door frames, siding, standing trees
1956 Ford pickups
placed in the palm of sling shots
landing in onion, corn fields, front yards
amid newspapers, stacked one foot high
clay flower pots, pincushions
someone's head, playing cards that folded
until the sound of trains had passed
neighbors climbed out of the ground.

Elizabeth J. Westrate

Great Blue Heron

She punches into sight
-my heart quickens-

fluid wings rise to the sky
& descend to bits of sun

sprinkled on the river,
I could have missed it

power pushing upstream
I could have had my eyes

turned down snuffing a
cigarette, instead I catch

a glimpse of her
as I sit in the rank air

of the car music beating
out of rhythm of my

heart music beating to
forget, quickly

she vanishes around the bend
-my heart quiets-

I light another cigarette
close my eyes.

Susan e. Pulju

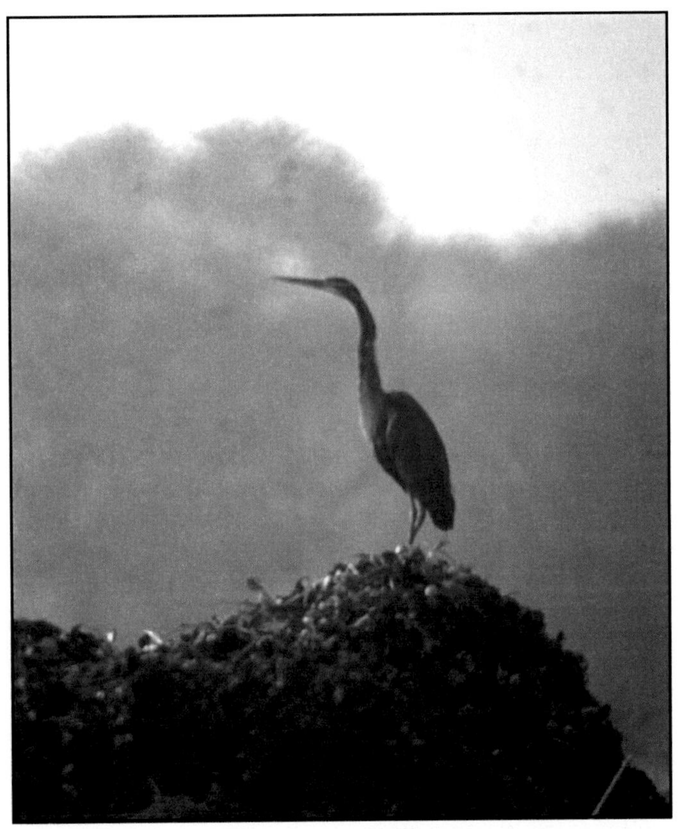

Patience, *Stan Woollams*

October 20

He's dead of course, and I killed him, then
took his breast and legs from inside his suit
the color of coins, pennies and doubloons

He was so brave, he ran so far with four shot
in his thighs, only the best of dogs could
find him, beak dripping red as the disks

around his eyes. I close his chest, fold
his wings, stroke his head greener than spruce
I weep. But I do not eat in ignorance

Jay Stielstra

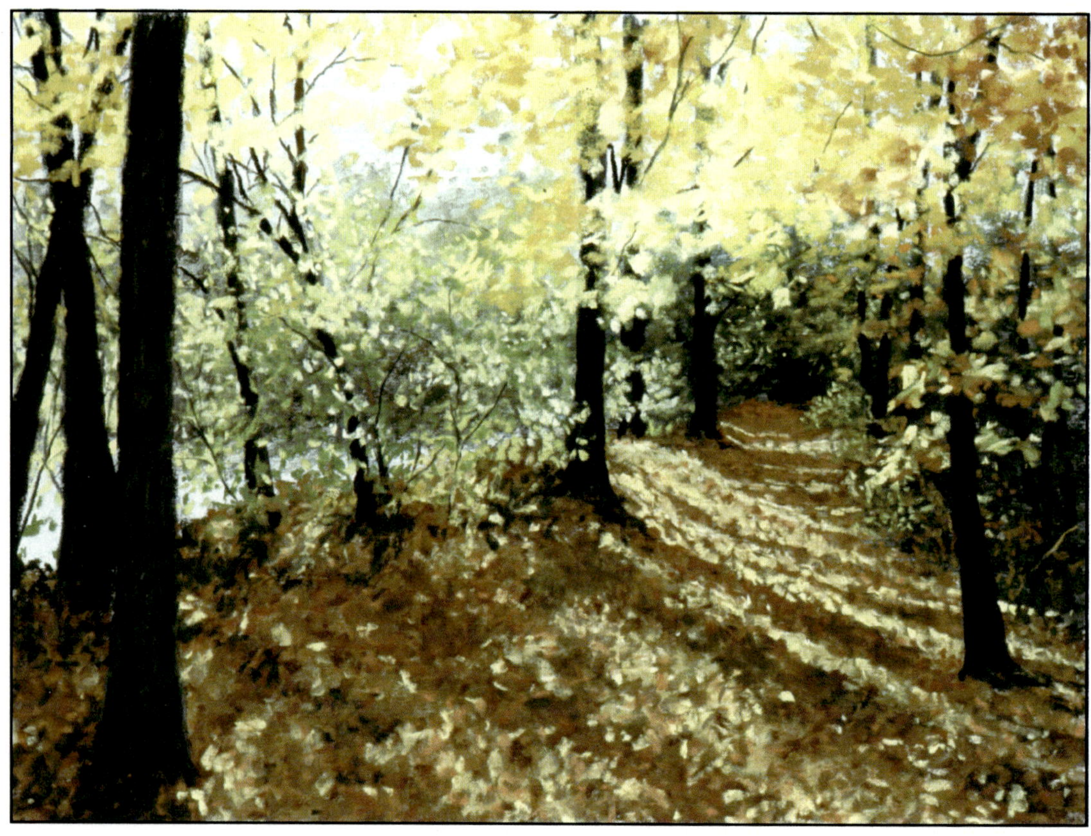

Untitled, *Laura Strowe*

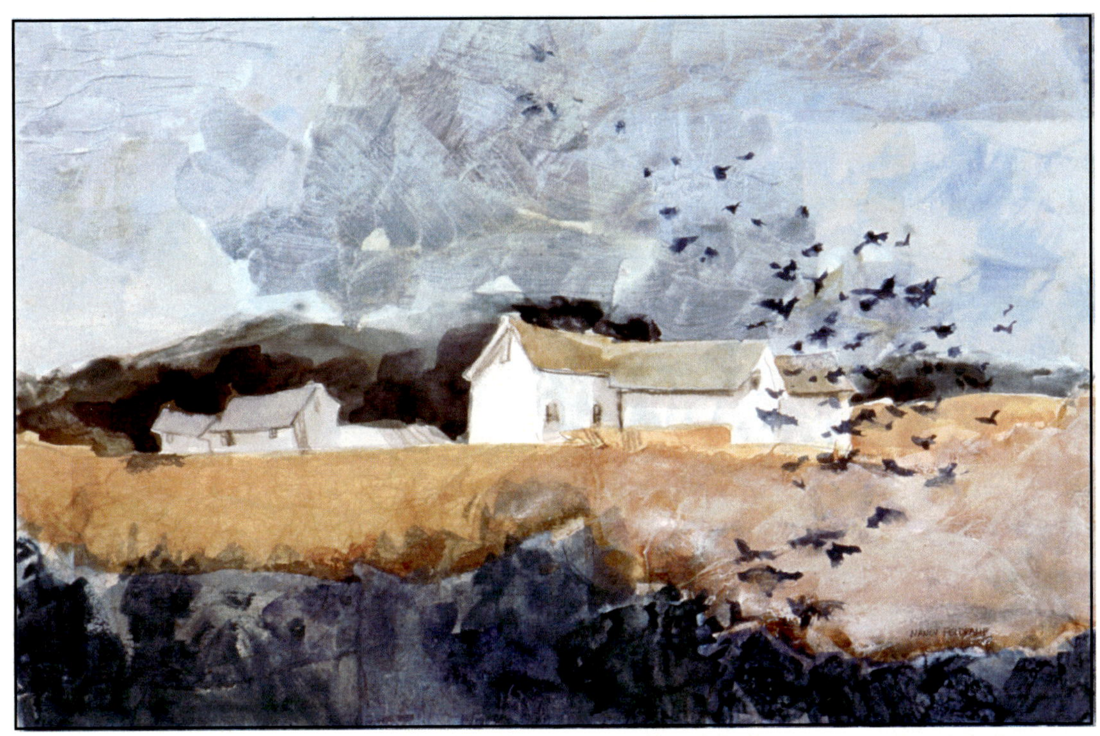

Flock of Blackbirds, *Nancy Feldkamp*

Roadkill

There are dangers to rural life that are not readily apparent.
For instance, I could be that dead deer lying akimbo
alongside the road. Today as I was stuffing the mailbox with
another do-not-send-me-this-stuff letter,
a maniacally driven white trashmobile whooshed violently by—
far too close, far too fast, far too much.
Almost roadkill, I glowered down the road hoping to cause
that sordid white vehicle to explode into moviemad flames,
lasering its thin tin hull into an irretrievable dimension,
retribution for reminding me that even the simplest act could
be my last, that even the humblest wishes cannot protect us,
that even clear sky days can be eternity's jagged edge.

Brad Tompkins

...cold air creeps out of the swamp...

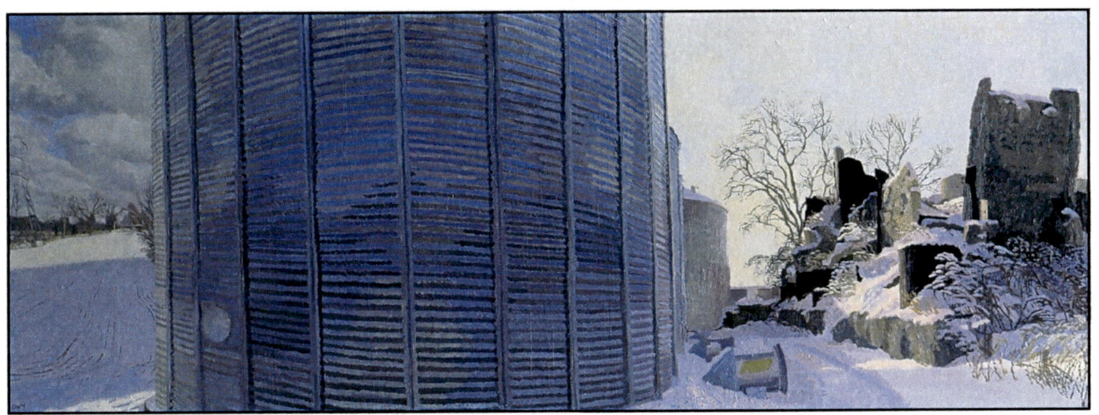

Silos at Solstice, *Elaine Wilson*

What We Bring to the River, What the River Brings to Us

Open-throated chuckle of a wood dove,
flow over flatrock   spruce branches sough,
        the regressive jug-jug of a bullfrog.
Then fish fins   evolved to the shape of the current,
        divide the ripples as a carp roots
    face-d   in the muck
                    wnriver from the Ford plant.
And sor   bscure splashes
                u can't see to assign meaning.

Cano   good kind) appear,
padd   rinting the stream with C's and J's,
            ces pitched at water temperature,
not   g above the birds' unceasing ostinato.

The river has breathed up to me
        old mustiness like air trapped in an antique drawer
and chilled me with its coolness
                    at the close of the hottest day.
I've walked by these waters in despair and abstraction,
I've brought my dailiness here,
I've made it my church.

May our chain-link demarcations never
                intimidate the river.
May our culverts never contain its waters for long.
May our chemicals cause no more than a blip
        in the life-graph of the smallmouth bass,
and the shells of endangered birds regain
                their power to nurture generations.
Let the river assimilate our broken-up pavement
                    into its pebbles
and wash away   with its gravity-drawn continuum
        every disturbance we bring to its banks.

Richard Tillinghast

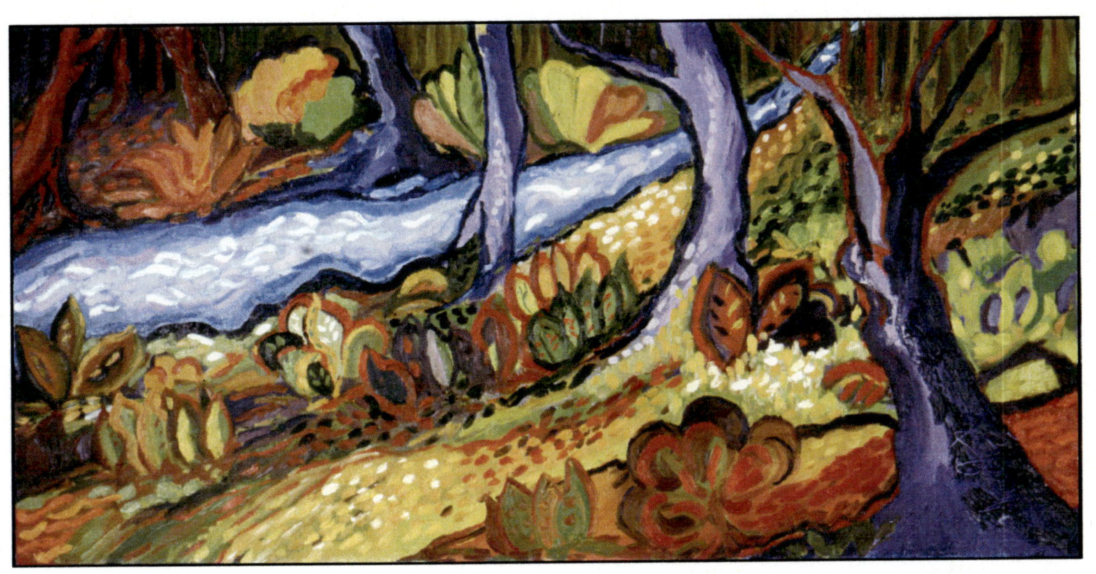

Spring River, *Ruth Gilmore Langs*

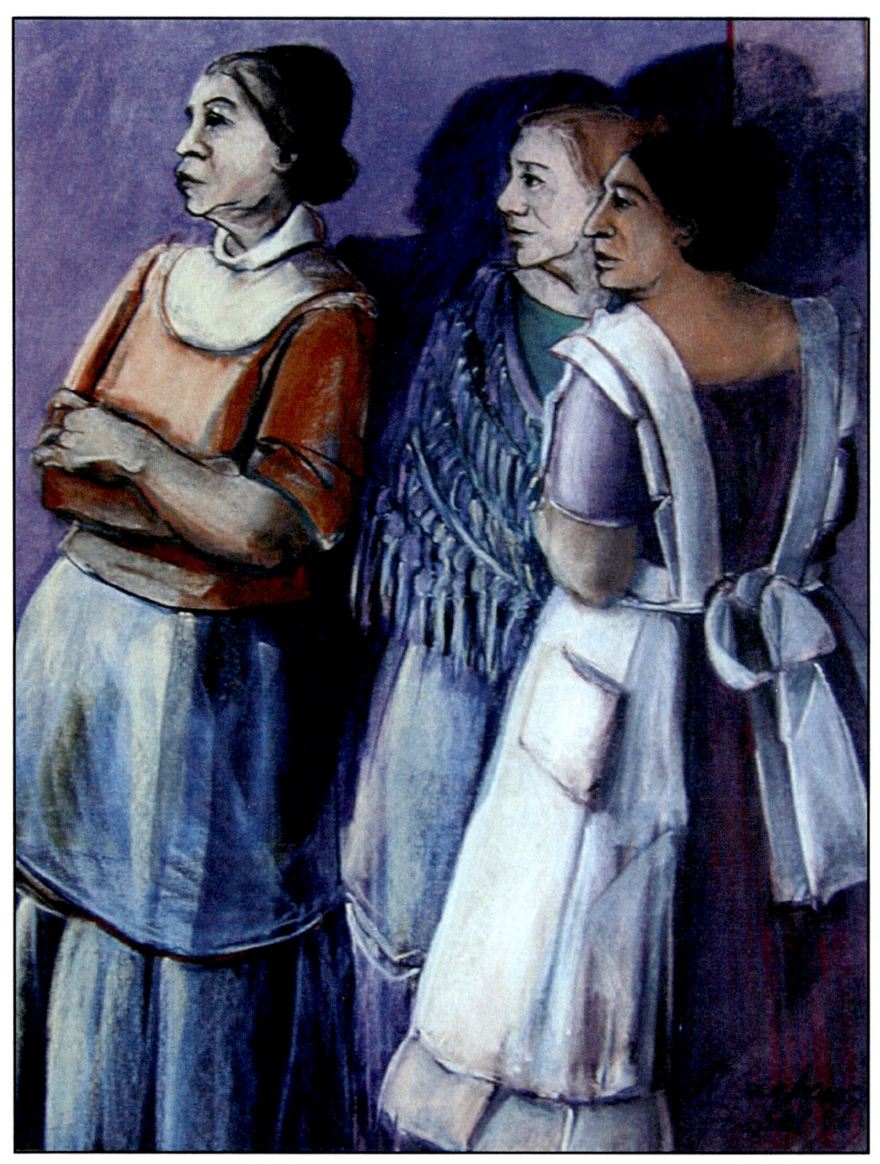

Three Women, *Meaghen Powell*

Nightime Trip to Migrant Camp on Esch Road, Manchester

Purple peach golden sunset
The migrant workers asleep
Beacons of light in tiny ramshackle houses glow in the
empty fields.
Darkness covers the garbage heaps, old ruins of trucks
and tractor parts left behind to rot.
The women and children wait for me
"La Guera" the light skinned one
and greet me shyly, quietly, respectfully in their language.
I want to shout in English
how I lost my way here in the dark
and knocked on strangers' doors looking for them.
They calm me with Spanish, and the moment
Their children playing at their feet
with puzzles, markers, crayons and paper
The TV on, Spanish soap operas
The sofa is soft and comfortable
The room simply clean
Cupboards covered by cotton fabrics
We eat salsa made at my home
only six miles away yet separated by oceans
of fears, differences, misunderstandings and
opportunities
My children will go to college
Yours will be lucky to finish high school
and blessed if they can find a new skill
You have been returning for fifteen years to this place
In four short weeks you will pack up your life and
migrate to Texas.
I ask "Will you return next year?"
You reply, "Dios sabe."
God knows
What do you do in Texas?
They sparkle, laugh and dream
We sleep in, relax, go out and enjoy ourselves, go to
Mexico
Children grasp the little books with their little fingers
I dream your babies will fall asleep to the tune of
mother and fathers' voices
reading "Buenas Noches Luna"
Goodnight Moon.

Carol Rose Kahn

Autumn

It should be nice to be forty
in October and know that someone
fell off a cliff with you
and never landed but hung
suspended, then stepped again
upon the brink, unwrapped
but walking, unchanged except
he loves you more now
that the leaves are falling

How's the Missouri look to you
Did Lewis and Clark pass through
near where you live now content
with nothing lost or lent
that could not later be returned
or have you spurned that denigration
yet and strive there still unwilling
to let those several oaken days of
summer slip ephemerally away
now that the air is chilling

Once I wrote of you
"slender as a whistle..."
You said to me
"remember when the train passes..."
It passed today, dog-whistle thin
and empty as a howl
I saw us walking palm to palm
near fat black oaks and in my throat
I knew that I would die
without forgetting

Jay Stielstra

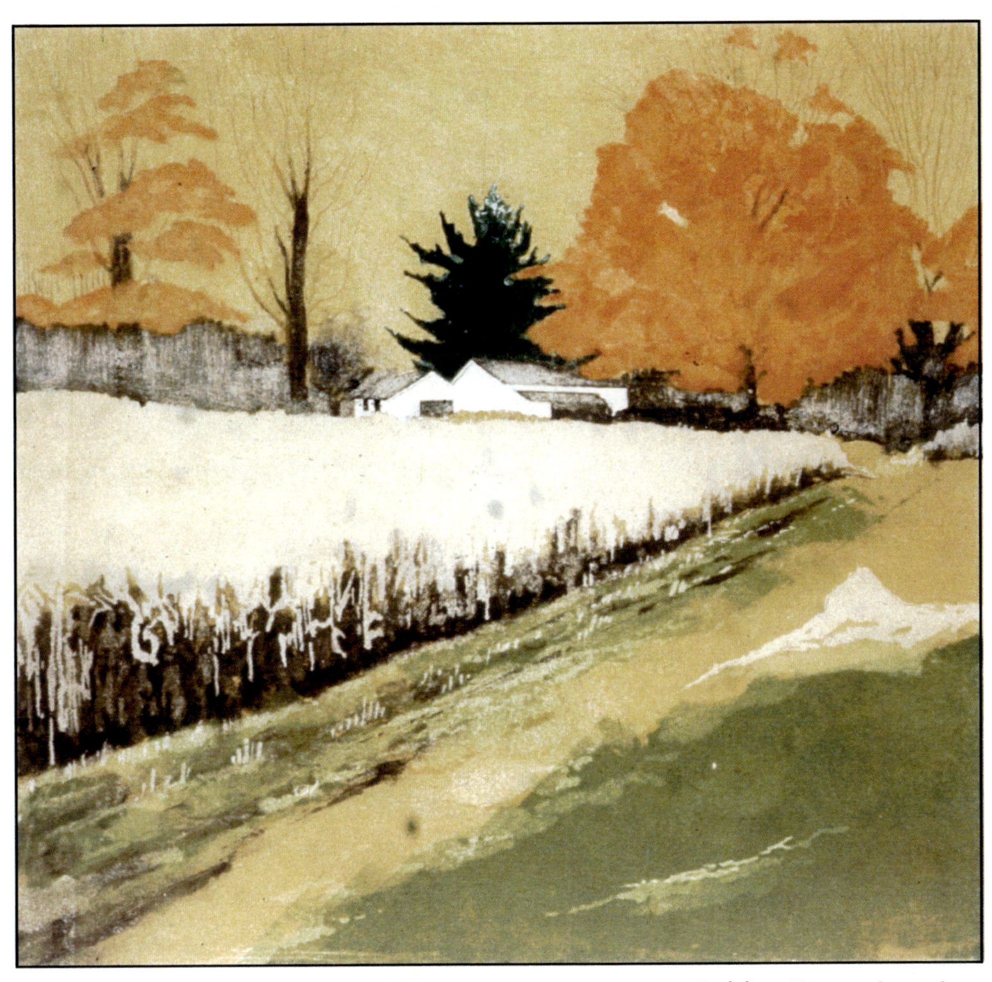

Golden Days, *Jean Lau*

A Pilgrim's Progress

During summer solstice
purple vetch and blessed thistle
spill over fields following vapor trails
and all the summer grasses:
sedge, wild oat, reed, and redtop
freed from the restraints of convention
fly free in the breeze.

It is then that I wind my way like a pilgrim
on the road to Waterloo and Chelsea,
to the cabin in the woods where my uncle
lives surrounded by his garden,
where bees swim from poppy to foxglove
while baby grapes form tiny button bodies
like coral colonies of a family matrix.

My uncle makes a pot of green tea,
the same he drank as a boy.
He remembers his trip to Mt. Rushmore
in 1937, sixty-three years ago this week.

He was a boy of nineteen,
setting out from Ann Arbor
in a Model A with his best friend Bill,
leaving a compact, self-contained town
perched on hills above the Huron River,
for vast open spaces, of grasslands, buttes and bluffs,
for mesas long deserted by Indian tribes.

On this adventure, crossing the Mississippi,
they sleep in cornfields, pass places
with names like Shawnee and Winnemucca.
They sip lemon cokes in a small town called Las Vegas.

Chosen like any young men
with a destiny on the eve of World War II,
they are called to view the mysteries
of mountains, deserts, the Pacific Ocean,
to proclaim the magnificent works of God and man.

In San Francisco, the Golden Gate Bridge
spans the harbor like a torii, gateway to heaven.
In Arizona, the Boulder Dam nears completion

water flooding the valley, gold rock slipping
below the cold blue surface of Lake Meade.

In Sundance, Wyoming, an aluminum wall
surrounds the town like a glistening medieval
fortress designed to hold back frenzied
plagues of locusts feeding their way cross country.

On roads through the badlands, deserted homes
mark the path of farmers chased away
by dust storms threatening to swallow them alive.
Nature, like the spirit of lost buffalo,
challenges a nation's industrial progress.

My uncle reflects on the mystery of it all.
Standing on the back porch under the shadow
of spruce and pine, he wonders how
particles of the Dust Bowl found their way to Africa,
a bit of Dorothy and Auntie Em on the Gold Coast,
and the same jet stream returns to us
carrying sands from the Sahara
depositing them half-way
around the world in our backyards.

Marijo Grogan

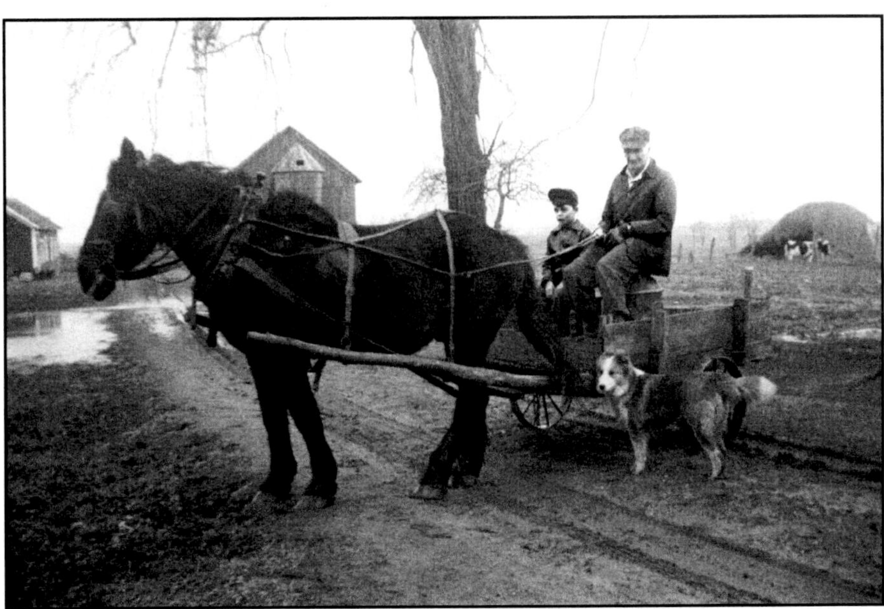

Pa, Sonny and Horse, *Mildred Dowling Clark*

Once

It pours out, the summer.
          This morning we woke cold
on the sleeping porch, smelling woodsmoke.
I dreamed that the poker-faced jacks and queens and kings
from our low-stakes summer games stepped
                  out of their one-dimensionality
and slashed at each other with cardboard swords.

The summer drains away somewhere
inside the hard inner tissue of trees.
The island in midstream—grassy, wildflowery—
dries to a patch of straw.

It's goodbye to the list that begin "a pair"
and ends "straight flush."
Goodbye to the bird book and the
                  Book of Michigan Wildflowers
          and the book of stars.
Goodbye to the moon that inflamed
          the crazy pack-music of coyotes.

The rough-legged hawk, and the branch he lit on
across the river from me our last morning:
my effort to hold completely still
while I brought the field glasses into
          focus on his beak,
and his eyes like twin vendettas;
the night four fives beat a royal straight in the last hand—
          those moments

                        are absorbed
into something called "yesterday,"
 "last week," "last month," "last summer,"
becoming at last a birdlike speck inside the cloud
that sails massively away behind us—

a glimmer, something unplaceable,
a brushstroke of sunlight on a screen
          in the memory of one of our children
from a time we lived happy in the full day.

The barred owl in the woods on the other
          bank of the river called,

and I heard his flourish of eight notes in the dark
for the first time in my life,
          and maybe never again.

Those clouds this morning that mount
          stratum by stratum higher
behind a wind out of Canada
will never configure themselves the same
               way again, ever.

Our dreams, the hands that were dealt us,
wherever it was the hawk's
          hunt took him that August morning,
whatever drew the owl into earshot that midnight—
none of this will repeat.

Everything only happens once.

Richard Tillinghast

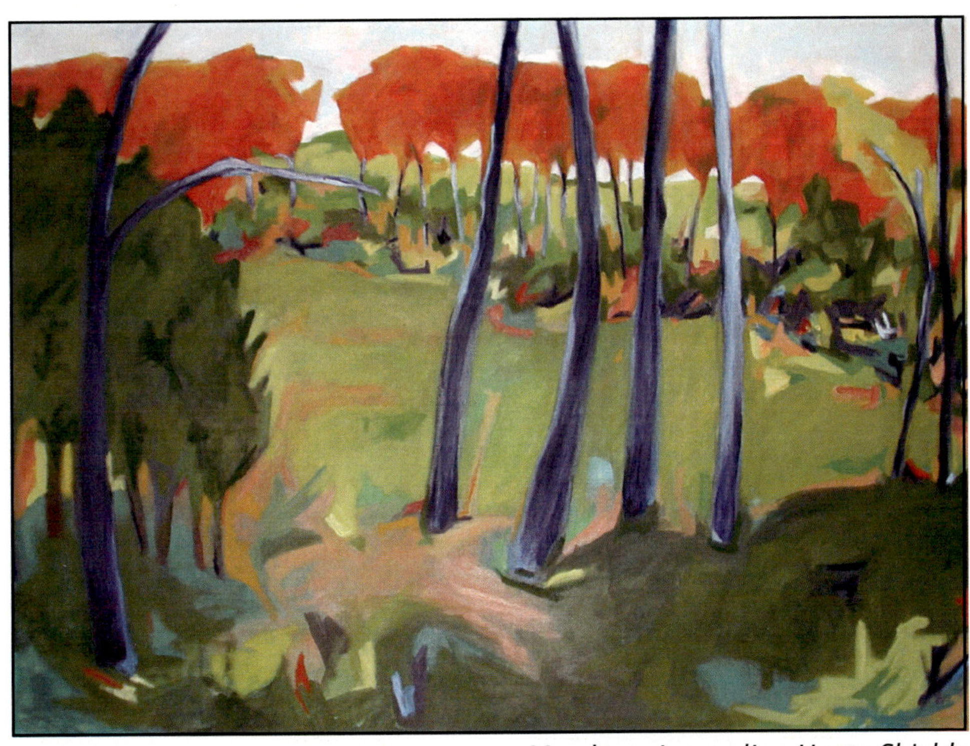

Meadow, *Jacqueline Hoats Shields*

...one hundred shades of white...

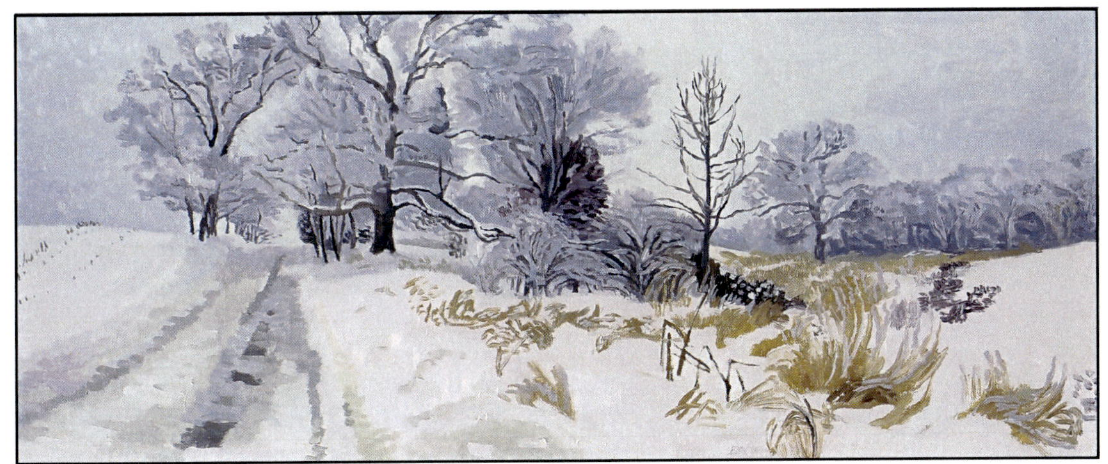

Hoarfrost on Lima Center Road, *Elaine Wilson*

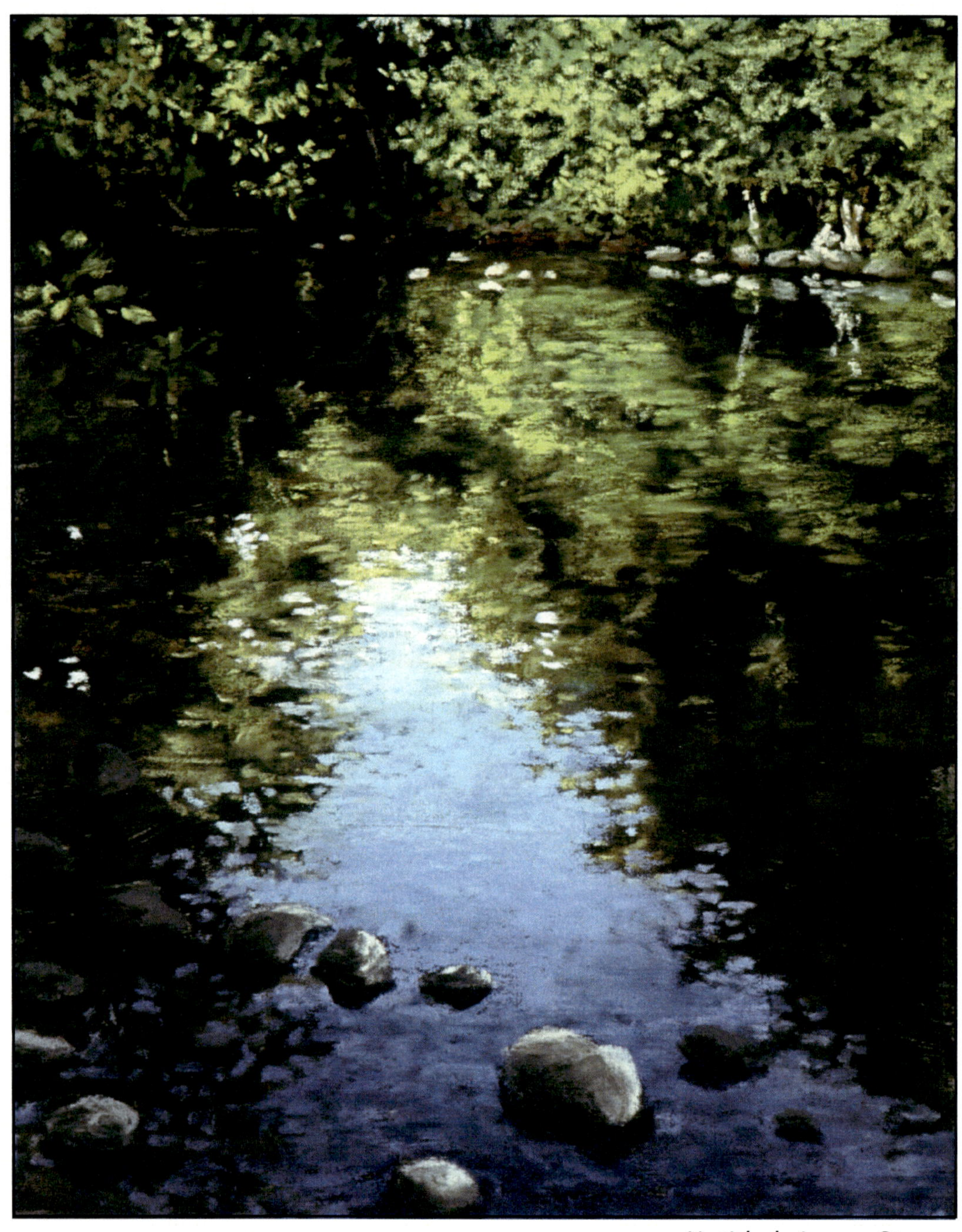

Untitled, *Laura Strowe*

Map

I would map the millpond
in a series of blue triangles
white ovals
the surrounding green shape
similar to paper left
on a set of stickers
after the stickers have been removed.
Similar to Monet's vision of sunlight
when his pond or river
turned into brush strokes
of red, yellow, and white.

The same map techniques apply
to timber bridges, concrete sidewalks
tops of trees, and words
in a single word
blue pond, circle, left or right
there may be one hundred words
one hundred shades of white
mixed with black and green in blue.
One hundred sizes, imperfections in a circle.
One hundred ways to turn right or left
by matter of degree
depends on your starting position.

And in one word I would hate myself
have no way to draw yellow.
But, in one hundred words
I find shades of myself to enjoy
highest rating, number ten
others a seven, drop to five
body parts that still rate a two or one
and in one hundred words
I may find yellow
inside my pants pocket
my mailbox. In the weather

Elizabeth J. Westrate

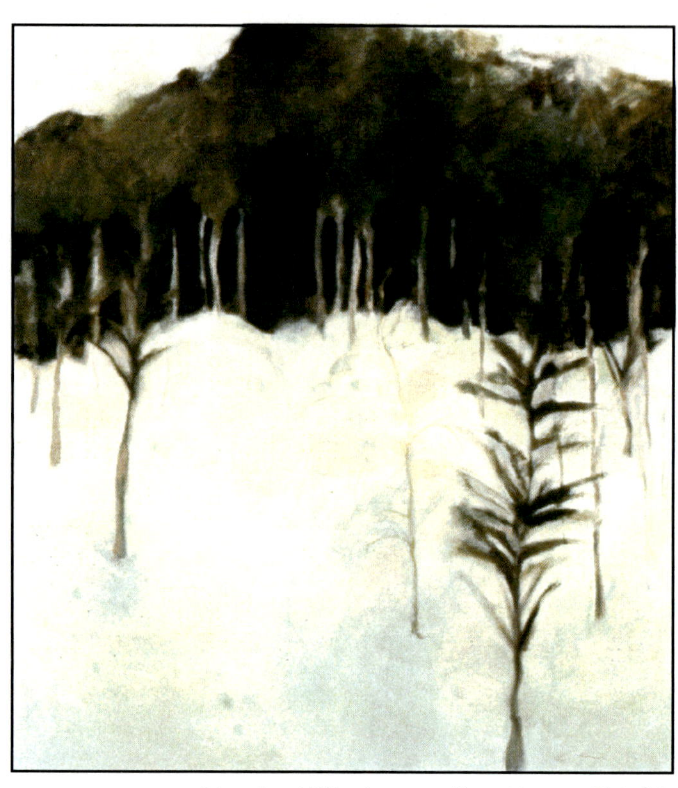

Up the Hill, *Jacqueline Hoats Shields*

Landscape, 1963: The Rocks

Maybe I was mooning over a girl…
I don't really remember…but I rode
out east of town to the Rosebud River.
It was just a stream, barely a yard wide.
I climbed through a fence, crossed a beaver dam,
and trudged up through poplars to a sandstone
outcropping: boulders and ragged pillars
weathered into hollows, cirques, hidden caves.
I leaned back against sandstone and looked out
across the valley into the evening.
A herd of mule deer? 6, 7, then 12
hopped up the hill, springing like cartoon deer—
did I know they could do this—until they
reached the fence at the top, just silhouettes
now against the evening sky, gracefully
hopping outlines easily vanishing
between the last barbed wire fence and the sun.

Keith Taylor

32

There is dirt under
My fingernails—
In spite of my aversion
To blind crawling creatures
I continue to work the earth—
The subtle beauty of the
Landscape enshrouds me
And
Like the flowers
I turn my face
To the sun

Melody Vassoff

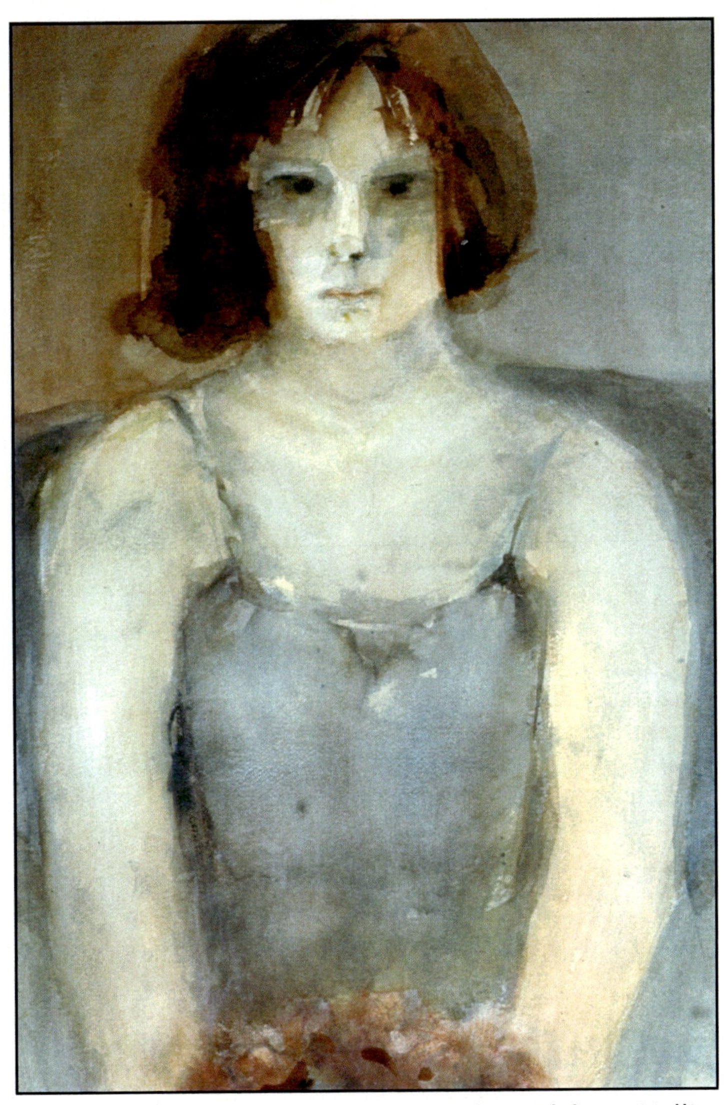

Flowergirl, *Madeleine Vallier*

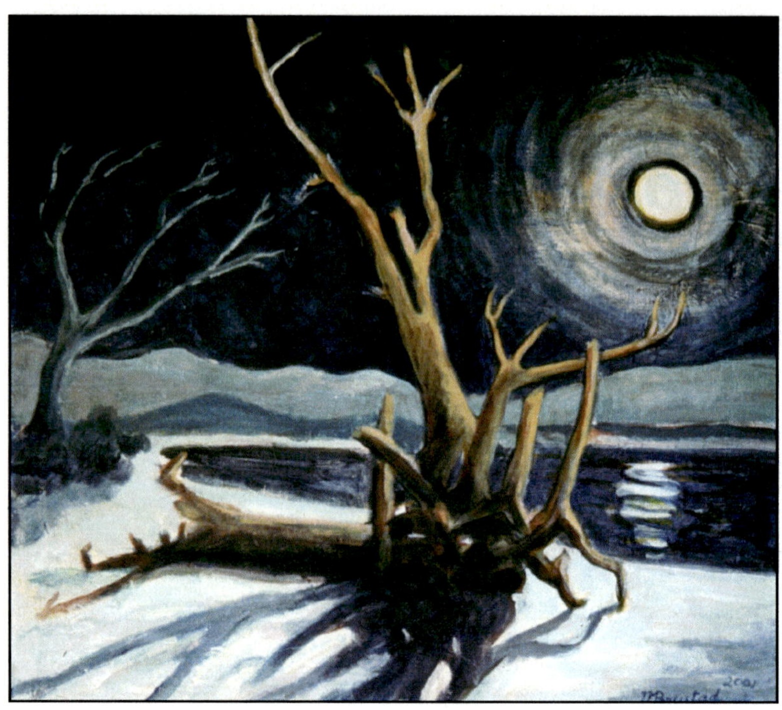

Moonstruck, *Ilona Brustard*

Vigil

Rose, you are the winter oak
whose spent leaves redden and remain
limp emblems of the heart's accustomed hold
on this—the known life of seasons,
daylights, nightfalls, weathers—
the ordinary calendars, mean time.
Ordinarily we live our lives out
hopeful and afloat among the rounded metaphors:
seedtime and harvest, dark and dawn;
solstice and equinox, calm, storm.
Ignoring the linear paradigms we move
buoyantly between our pasts and futures
gamely trading prospects for remembrances,
deaf to the regular changing of tenses—
those doorways slamming down the narrowing hall.
Behind the doors, we hear the voices still:
Goodnight. Godspeed. God Bless. Get Well. Goodbye.
The deaths we seldom grieve but set our watches by.

Thomas Lynch

34

You are the dark
Garden of
My soul
Only within
Your indistinct
Yet tangible
Boundaries
Can my spirit flourish
Nourished by
The rich
Earth
And
Surrounded
By wild beauty

Melody Vassoff

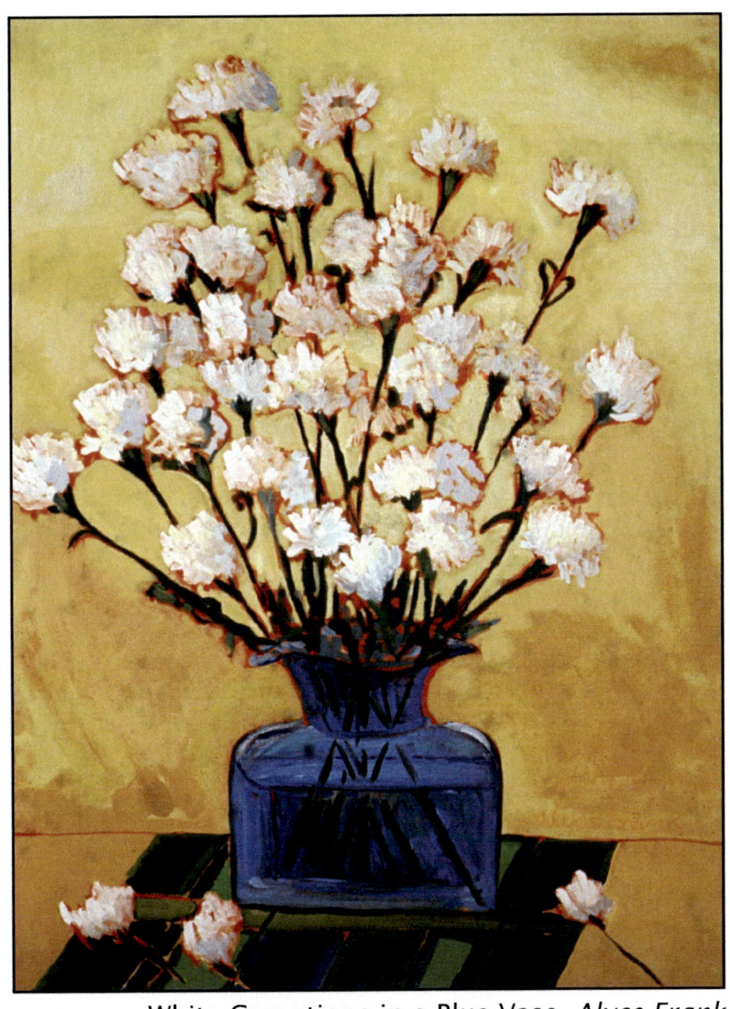

White Carnations in a Blue Vase, *Alyce Frank*

Sandra, Meet the Moon

Looking over my shoulder at the moon
Framed by a window in the clouds
I thought how like you it was last night
A magnificent celebrity
Appearing in the summer sky
A few brief moments, then fading out
Leaving the lighting to fireflies
And the occasional star.

We walked the road at midnight, you and I
So many times
Crunching the gravel and listening to
Creatures scuttling in the dark
Trains whistling across the river,
Discussing our fathers, our work,
Our hidden secret selves
As lovers often do.
Totally focused on ourselves
As children often are.
When you first saw the moon each night
You bowed to it and owned it
Introducing us (Sandra, meet the moon)
Like guests at a party
Who had never met before.
And we hadn't—not like that.

Walking the road alone last night
Looking over my shoulder
I notice the moon looks older
Since you've gone.

Sandra Xenakis

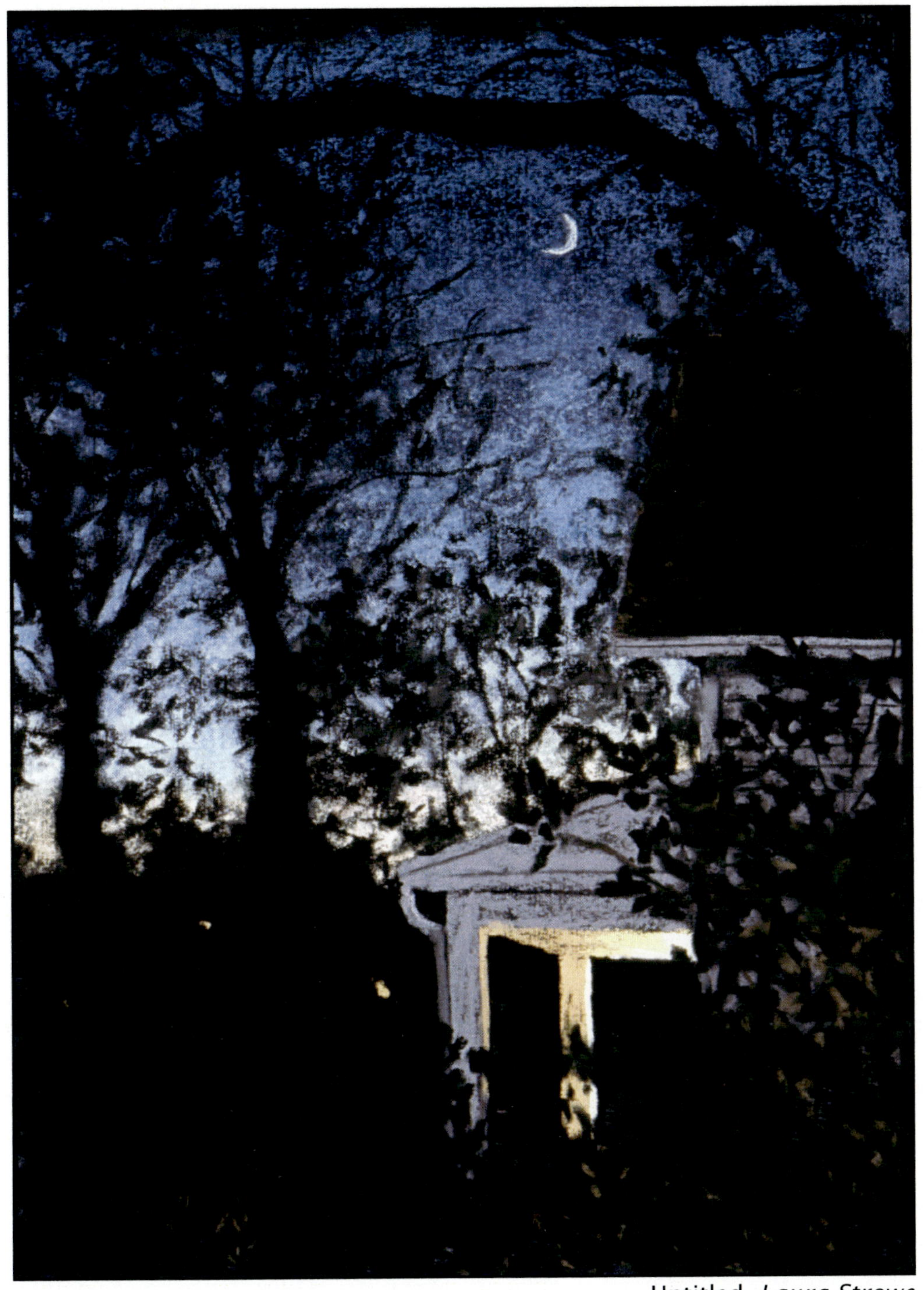

Untitled, *Laura Strowe*

...what will we eat when the last farm dies...

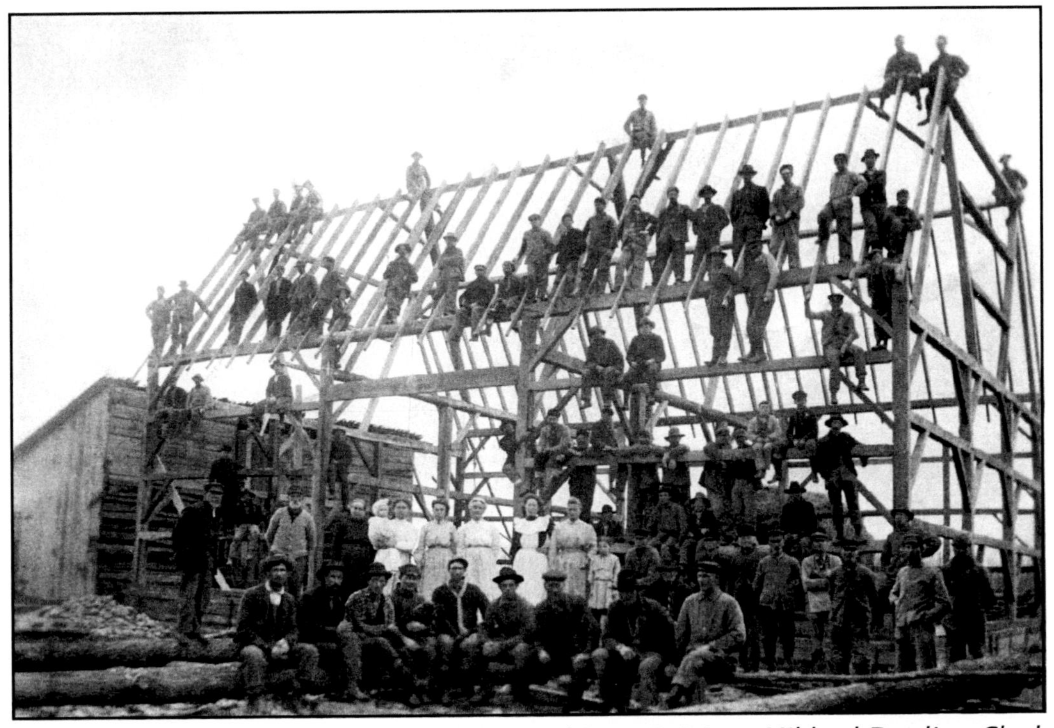

Ayers' Barn Raising, *Mildred Dowling Clark*

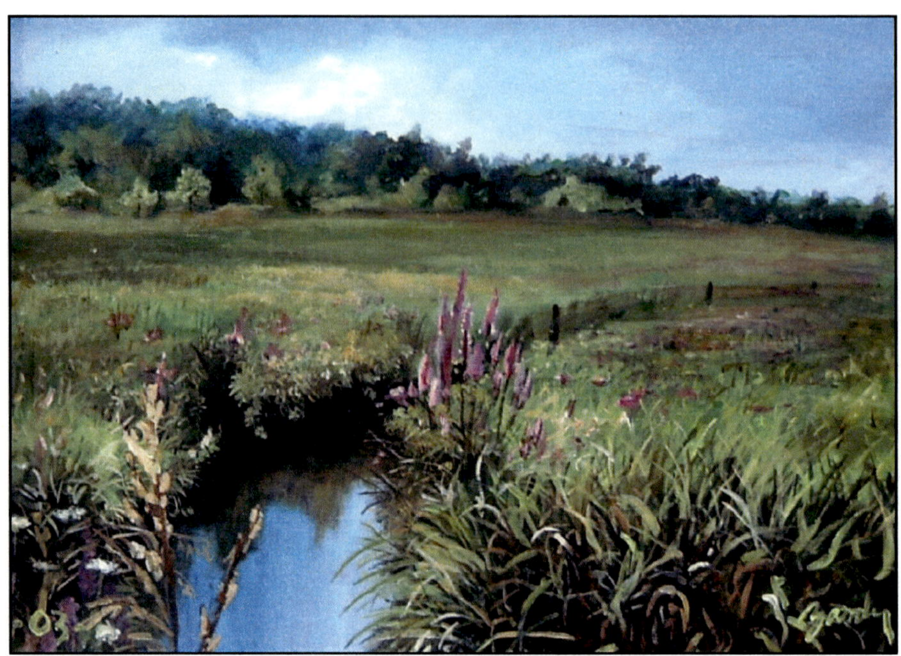

Eaton Road, *William Brody*

The Moment

Do you see it when it goes?
That moment when nature yields to the hand of man
Infinite yet delicate systems collapse into the mundane
Wildlife become as pet or vermin depending on the season

Rivers are choked to idleness to meet our manifold desires
Our lives spill out into our water and wood and overwhelm them
We got the numbers and in the end numbers drive it all
They say "you can't just slam the door," at least they could knock

Does it matter that a child can grow up and not know what it is to be wild?
Wilderness of spirit and wilderness of action, we have made these things taboo
We acknowledge the wilderness of the land and the spirit, yet seek to define, con-
fine it
The wilderness sells trucks to those who will never go there, beer to those who
can't.

We approach a point of control over our environment, pyrrhic as it may be
I miss the corn trails down the roads, the solitude, the wild
The moment approaches, heralded by innocuous events
When it passes will we know, will we tell our children what they cannot have?

Oscar Marx

40

death of the hired tractor

blue and white tractor decapitates tender lawn,
whirring blades freeing blades thick from tree shade,
the Ford circles this verdant carpet,
a renewable blanket riddled with holes and
bare shoulder patches that resist any shawl at all,
as fierce roots jut up defiantly.
all winter this tractor, freezing and unheeded,
idly awaited spring,
its original owners gone to cancer,
long past its zenith and
pining to do its mulish duty,
its steering in need of severe correction,
belts, pulleys, and bearings crying for balm,
for the unguent of ingenuity and divine intervention
and instead, true to its desire to serve,
struggles one last time around the familiar ground,
cracks a casing on a brutal branch and
spills its guts on a half mown lawn,
dying dignified in labor's savage harness.

Brad Tomkins

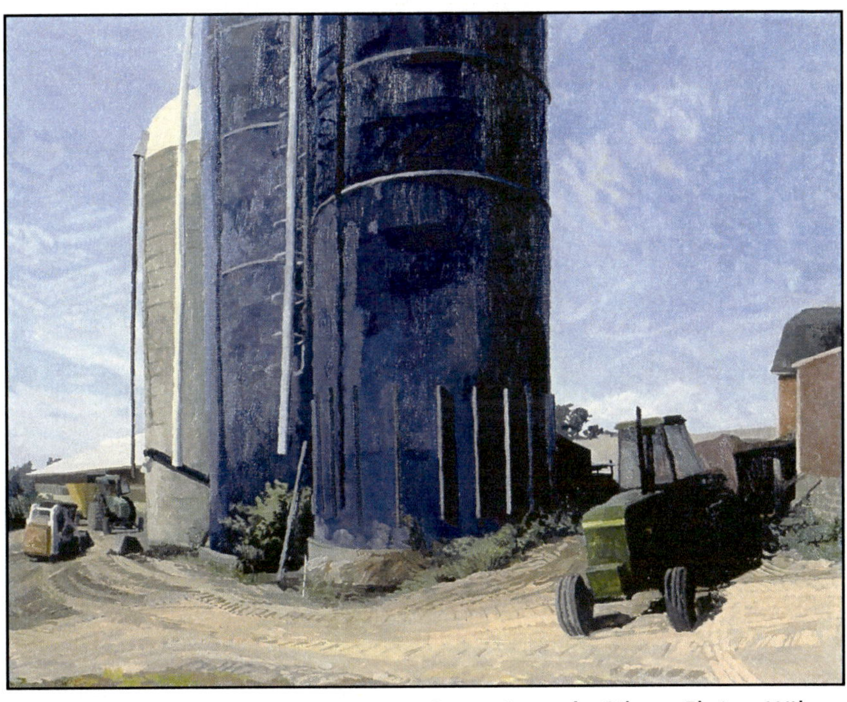

Breuninger's Silos, *Elaine Wilson*

Missionaries On The Porch

Taking a nap, adrift in a shallow dream,
the door bell rings. Children gallop to
the door. Under their heavy feet floors
creak like old bones breaking, walls and
hallways tremble. I crawl to the window
and pull my numb body up over the sill.
Missionaries are standing on the porch.
The shine off the two young men dressed
in black pants and starched white shirts
stirs up the rotten chunk of potato eaten
for lunch, spawns visions of my brother
the hunchback spying from high atop
a famous Parisian cathedral.

Over the long whine of the door opening
I hear my daughter invite the evangelists in.
"Dad, there's someone here to see you."
So much for fatherly advice about never
talking to strangers. Have they not heard
the thunder, these Christian Soldiers
loitering on the landing? Can the two
be so enchanted they don't feel the rain
on their skin when the rest of us have
developed a nervous tick after bullied
this long under a ruthless downpour?
I pull on my shorts, slip on a T-shirt and
stumble down the stairs in my bare feet.
"Can I help you?"
"We'd like to help you brother, achieve
a personal relationship with your Lord."
I tell them thanks, but I've been breaking ice
in the marsh all spring preparing the water for
cranes to nest among the fallen twisted cattail,
and that's as close to meeting Jesus as I'm
likely to get.

My stirring liturgy startles the cat on the end
table into a hasty retreat, kicking over a glass
of milk with his paws as he leaps. Instead of
being run off from boredom or disgust,
the boys sing me a hymn—
        Come, thou long ex-pected Lord,
        Born to set us free, from our fears
        And sins release us, let us find
        Our rest in Thee!

This is why we build houses a half mile off
the road behind twenty acres of marsh and
woods, to pick tomatoes in our underwear
and stare out over green rolling hills for days
listening to frogs mate until our ears fall off
from the joy.   And still they come.

"I don't mean to be rude brothers, but so much
vertical H2O makes a person melancholy,
and to be honest, all the love I can spare today
is upstairs looking for stars in broad daylight
—imagine— with the binoculars I gave the kids
the day their big yellow dog came up lame and
couldn't chase them out through the weedy
alfalfa fields anymore."

Watching the righteous walk back up my long
gravel driveway under a cloudless late Spring
afternoon sky, I wonder why it matters to them
what we believe. As long as we keep our
promises, most of the time, and are there with
a warm wash rag to wipe away the vomit from
our lovers' feverish lips, this should be enough
to get us into heaven or anywhere else with a
nice view, good neighbors and no money down.

Doug Smith

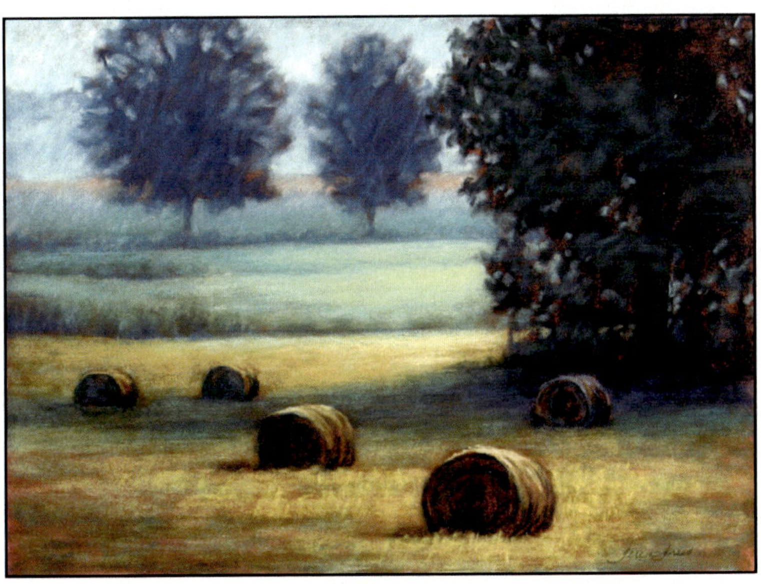

Haying Season, *Teresa Freed*

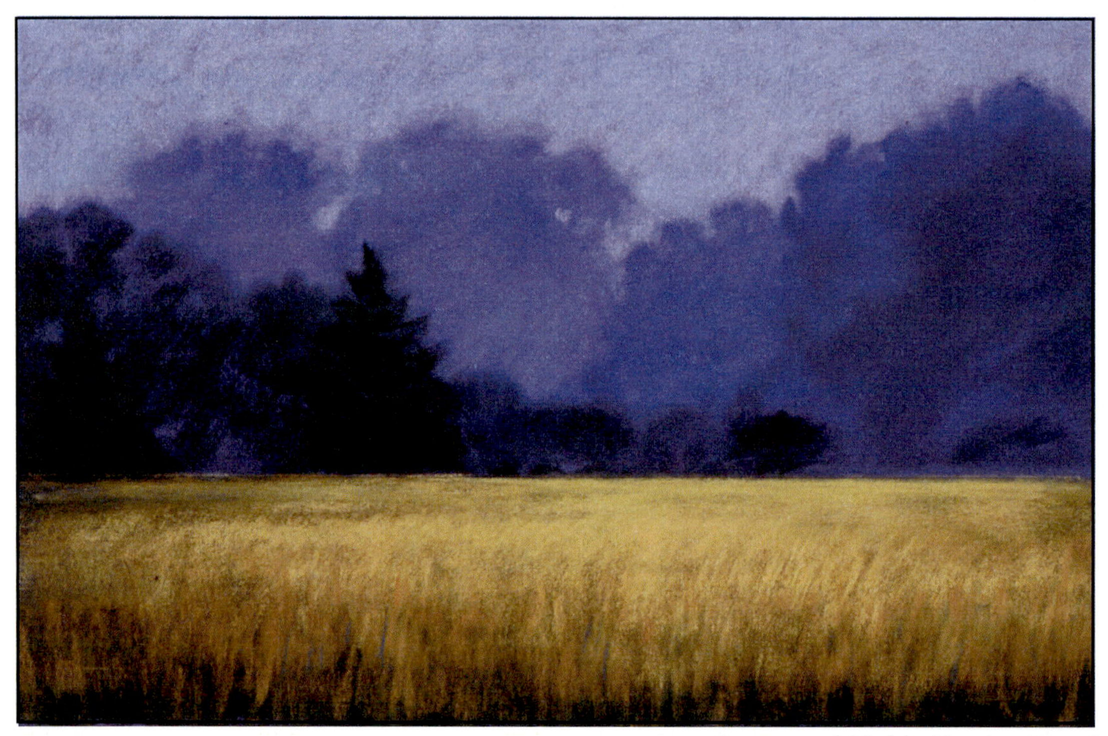

Rapeseed Field, *Teresa Freed*

The Rapture

The last frog of summer
sits under my window at night
calling in a loud insistent manner,
alarming me with her demands.

I wonder how she escaped the sweet chorus
of marsh frogs whose tribal chanting
lulled me to sleep on spring nights.
Those who sleep now in mud below.

Then there is a long silence.
A silence foreshadowing death
or a still winter landscape,
an empty tundra, this season without frogs.

As we drive along the autumn roads
you talk about conspiracies;
the government destroying small farms,
the farms being sold to developers.

I'm watching golden soybean fields
fly by.
I am thinking of the rapture
when in the last days of time
frogs and farmers will
feast together.

Marijo Grogan

Hungering for an Answer

what will we eat
when the last centennial farm
dies and is reborn
as a hundred brand new houses

will our children learn
to plant potatoes
harvest them
and store them properly

or continue as slaves
unknowing and serene,
consume what mighty giants
find most fit to feed them:

strawberries in January
bananas all year 'round
apples that Snow White
would fiercely refuse

II
who will love the soil
as the farmers do:
bow to the rising sun
listen for the stars
the rain, the wind
and kneel to the earth
<u>every</u> day, regardless of
the birds, the bugs
the heat, the drought
or an occasional wish
to send the cows
away to summer camp

III
who will love the farmers enough
to pose the Grail question:
what ails thee, brother?
as did Parzival, at last,
ask the Fisher King of old.

do we watch them:
sweat and toil,
pass sleepless nights
about the taxes,

wonder why they work so hard
and harvest such a long way off

do we wish them
any less good fortune
than babes fresh from the womb
teething upon silicon chips
who will, some future day,
dwell in a subdivision castle
atop a fertile funeral mound

IV
and once again I ask:

*what will we eat
when the last centennial farm
dies and is reborn
as a hundred brand new houses?*

Rosemary Caruso

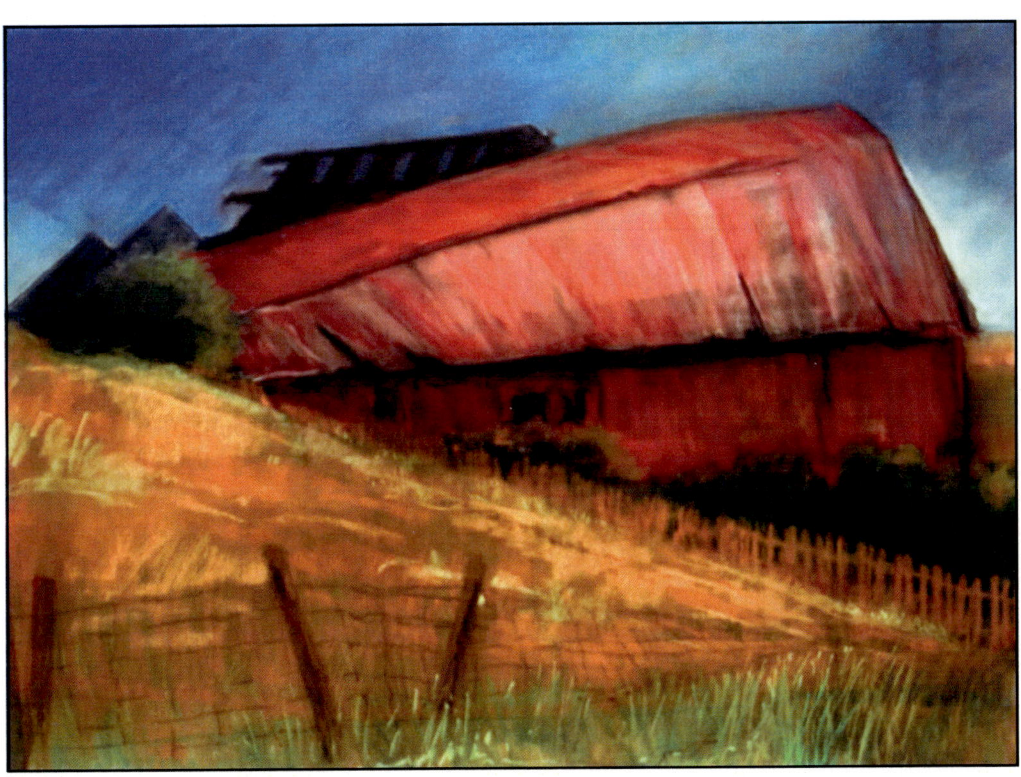

Fallen Icon, *Jean Lau*

...I can tell a green field from
a cold steel rail...

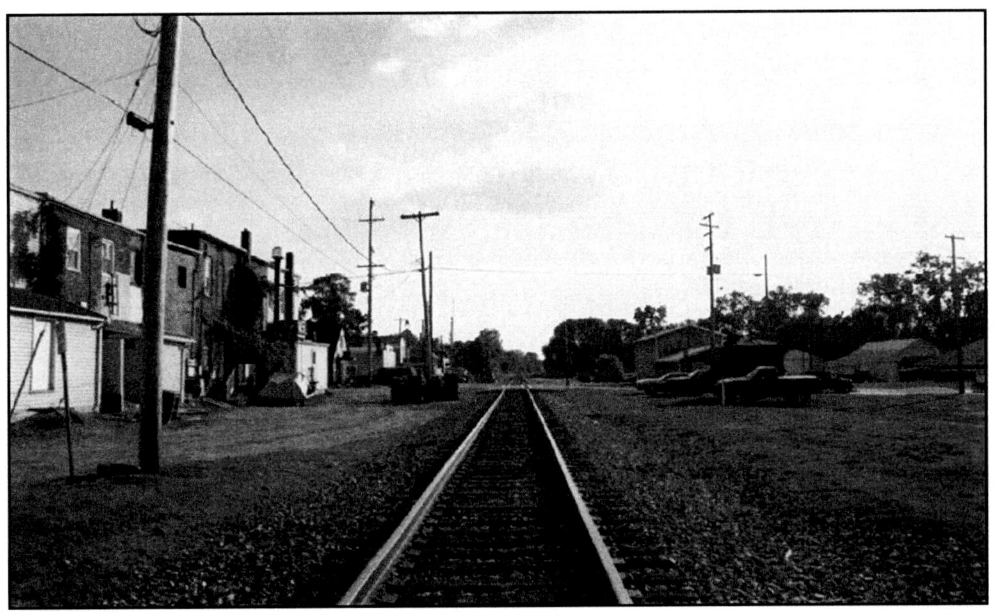

Tracks 2, *Alex Tinsley*

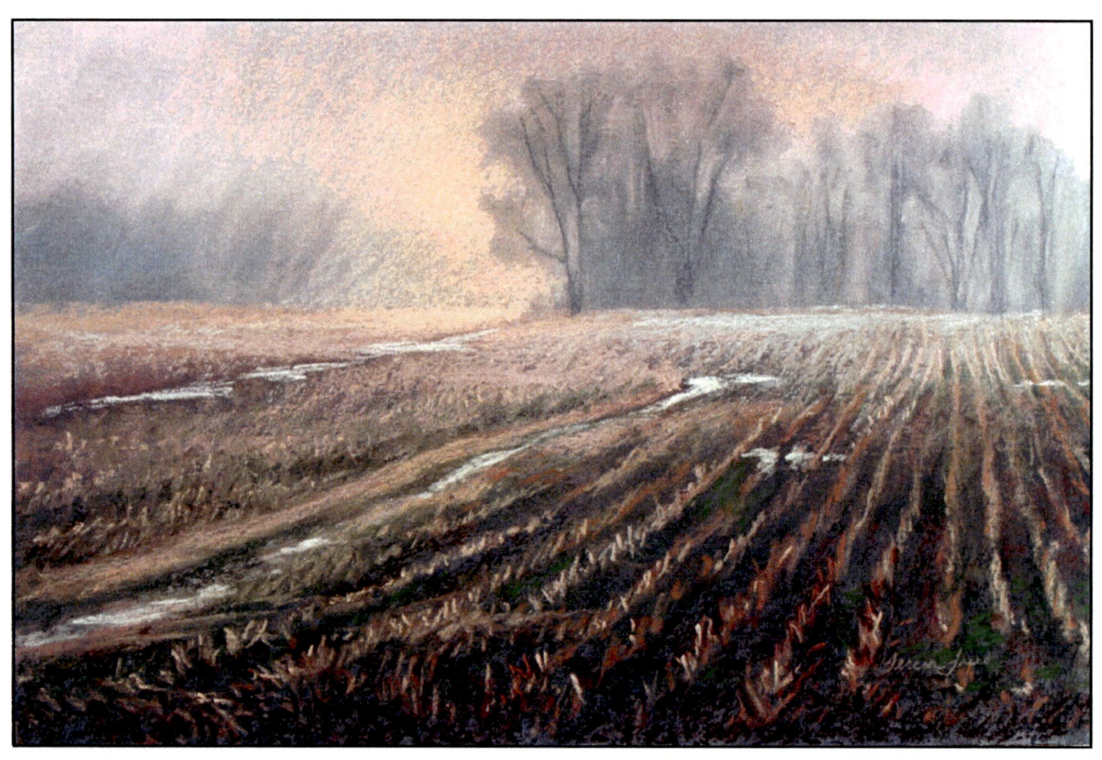

Spring Thaw, *Teresa Freed*

Sunday's Song

In the spring, the air is upside down.
Lima bean clouds slump over hungry trees,
and hard rains fall like bullets on a martyr.
Following a doe into the marsh
a middle-aged man trips over a root,
rolls down into the creek,
hears the low snore of frogs.
Faithless frost lingers in the numb ground,
as valleys choke on the river's bile.
He thinks he cannot bear to live
on this land through another summer.
Here, where gravity is a ruthless overseer
hiding in a thick fog. Hail and fallow skies,
soy bean bushes grim as barbed wire
for as far as the eye can see.

Driving the family to church,
the car hits a cat who disappears
under the wheels into the weeds.
Maybe it won't die, someone whispers.
Sprinting through the sanctuary doors,
his children kneel between two pews,
draw pictures of castles and dragons,
don't stand for the doxology,
wonder why their father never
puts money in the collection plate.
His wife listens for the punch-line
in the pastor's sermon.
First notes of a familiar hymn
lazily ascend from organ pipes
mounted on the wall under the cross.
Every believer rises.
The noise the congregation makes
is earnest but not quite pious.
He has to step away from her
when she is singing.

Doug Smith

Thirty Pounds

30 pounds of over-ripe bananas discovered at the bottom of the freezer!

> Frozen fetuses,
> twins triplets, single sacs of aborted promise
> never to generate from my hands into bread of good intentions.
> They only melt and ooze,
> sloughing off stillborn dreams.

What mad denial led me to stash 30 pounds of over-ripe bananas?

> Two, three, one, good for
> something I'll make up later.
> Warm lumps of bread to be my gifts—
> Wisps of air, fairly breathing,
> prove my care.

> How hard to throw away the promise.
> I struggle to admit the change; I cannot produce
> something lovely with these bananas.
> Blackened slugs trail paths to decay, signs of my neglect.
> Useless debris, discarded lumps, sweetness melts to nothing.

I ask for help, and we clear the freezer of 30 pounds of over-ripe bananas
to make room for

> second child's first deer.
> He's learning every path and habit,
> stalked the buck of branching grandeur,
> scoffs out loud, yet I've heard him murmur
> "Go in peace" when we pass road kill.

> "Not Bambi's father," he counters me,
> "we need the meat", cites population statistics,
> ponders suggestions to shoot the females.
> Veering between ego and necessity,
> he considers and cares.

> A small, sweet doe killed cleanly,
> two moments pause, he stops and thanks,
> "Go in peace, little one."
> The shot to her heart bruised much meat,
> the butcher chides us.

She yields to our need and offers 30 pounds exactly.

Hermione Miles Gorney

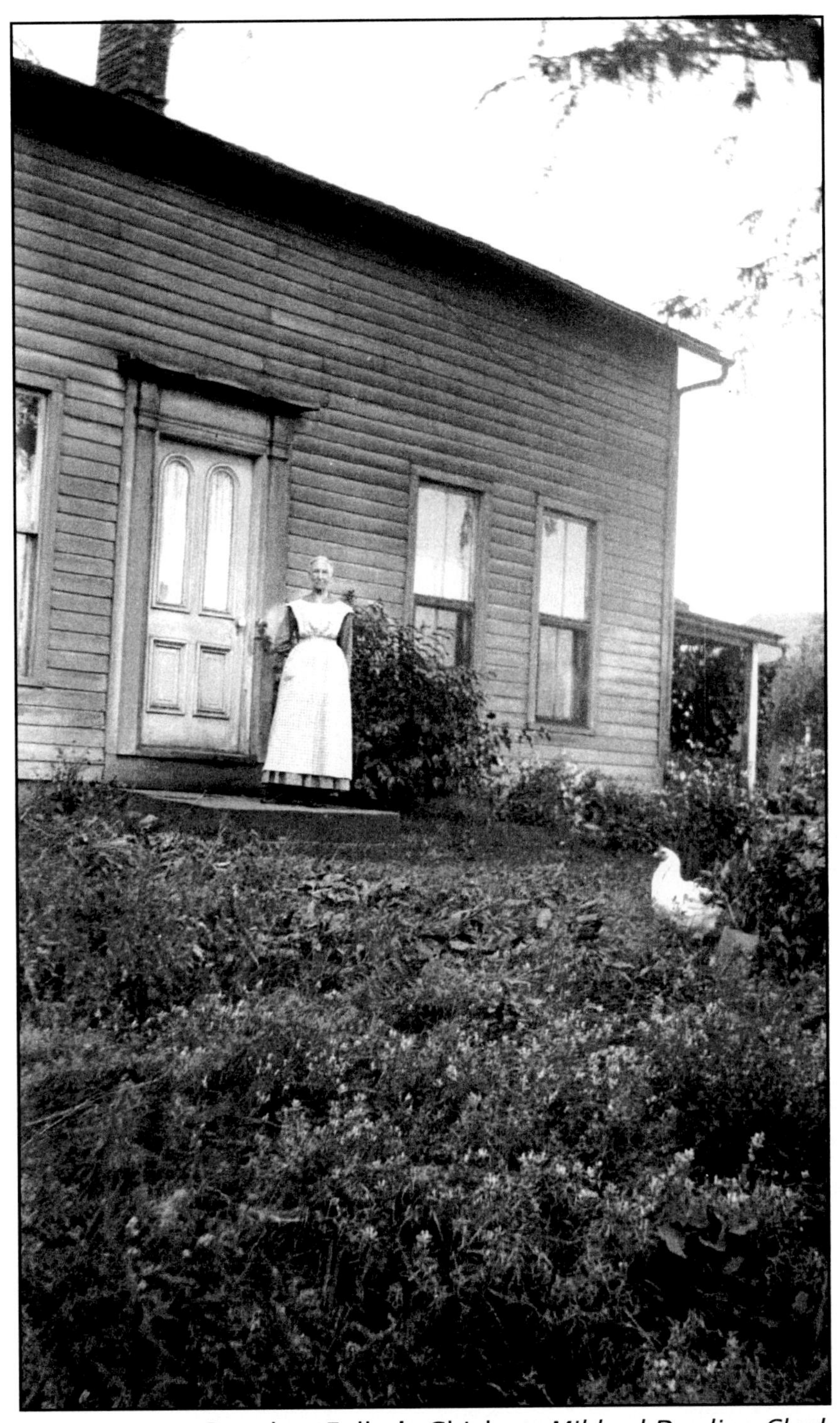

Grandma Fuller's Chicken, *Mildred Dowling Clark*

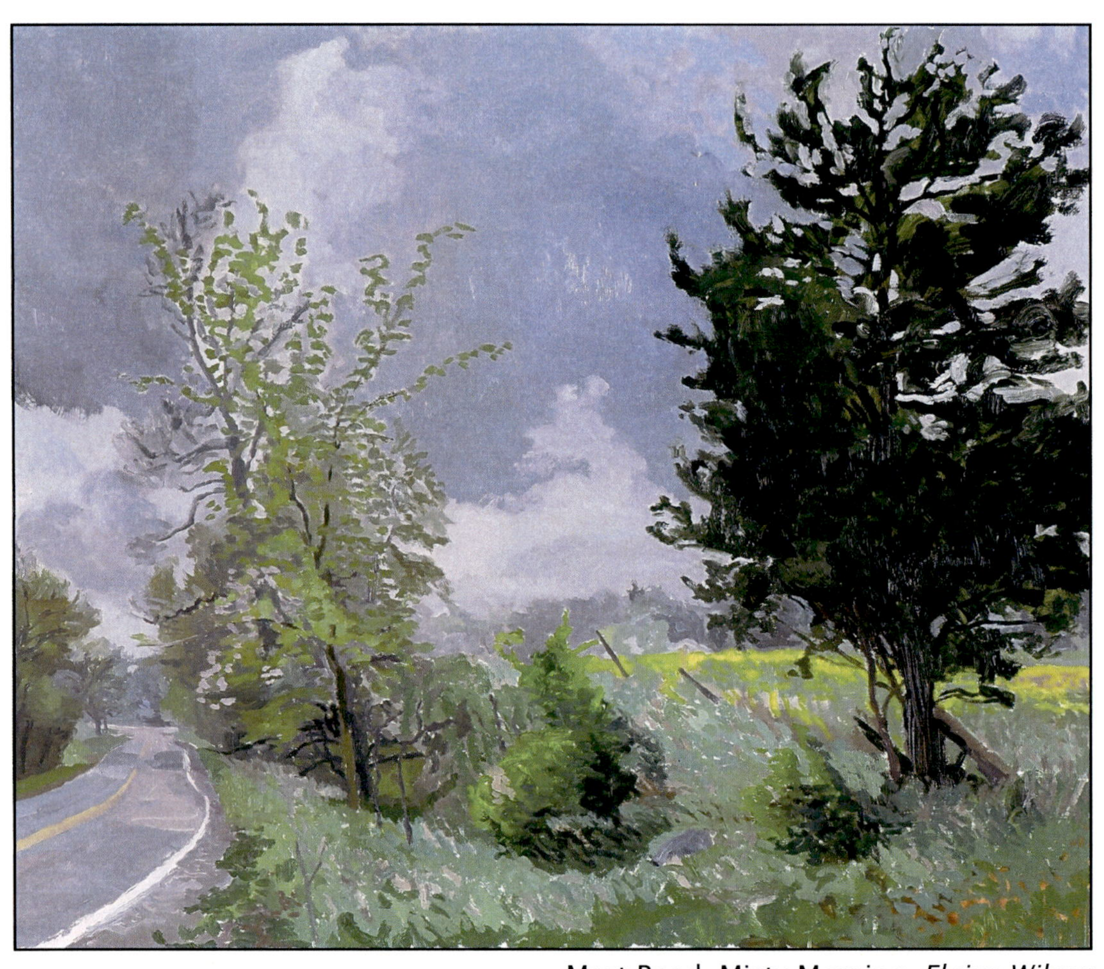

Mast Road, Misty Morning, *Elaine Wilson*

Waiting for Silence on North Territorial Road

Even in this place, nearly
hearing breezes
and colliding bird calls—
languages
written on
ancestral genes, my senses
fade under vague trees as my
eye tries to follow a butterfly's
erratic shifts.

Barely alive in a
derangement of culture.
My imagination's awkward
static in a strident
world where
silence is unheard of
as water spills
from taps returning
discolored to spongy earth.

A dull drone from the sky—
flight BA203, fifteen minutes
late landing at Detroit Metro.
My attention seizures as
fear, annoyance,
bewilderment flay
my fractured senses.

I am never home. All
longings are almost
lost among the railing
squads, the clutter, the
flurried movements
of accelerating civilization.
We cannot rest or
sleep, or stop ourselves.

Kent Ashton Walton

Farmer

He is of the earth.
Of long, holy days in meadowlark fields
Black soil in rolls against Spring sky,
The richness of sun-drenched hay.

With only love he lays his hands open
Strong, generous hands that hold
The freshness of Summer in an ear of corn,
Or the beaming faces of his beloved cherubs
Who frolic in the vastness of his humble garden.

David B. Sing

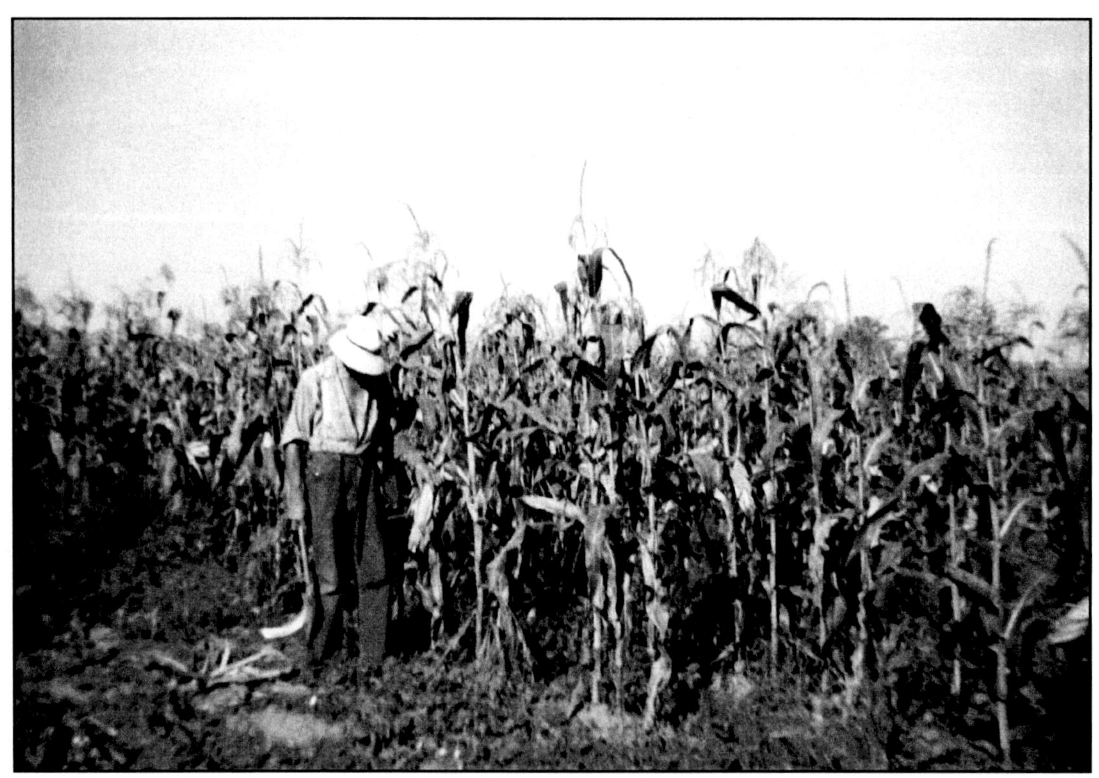

Pa in the Corn, *Mildred Dowling Clark*

Town

...They sat by a window that looked over the roof of a small frame building on Main Street. By turning their heads they could see through another window, along an alleyway that ran behind the Main Street stores and into the back door of Abner Groff's bakery. Sometimes as they sat thus a picture of village life presented itself to them.

Sherwood Anderson from Winesburg, Ohio

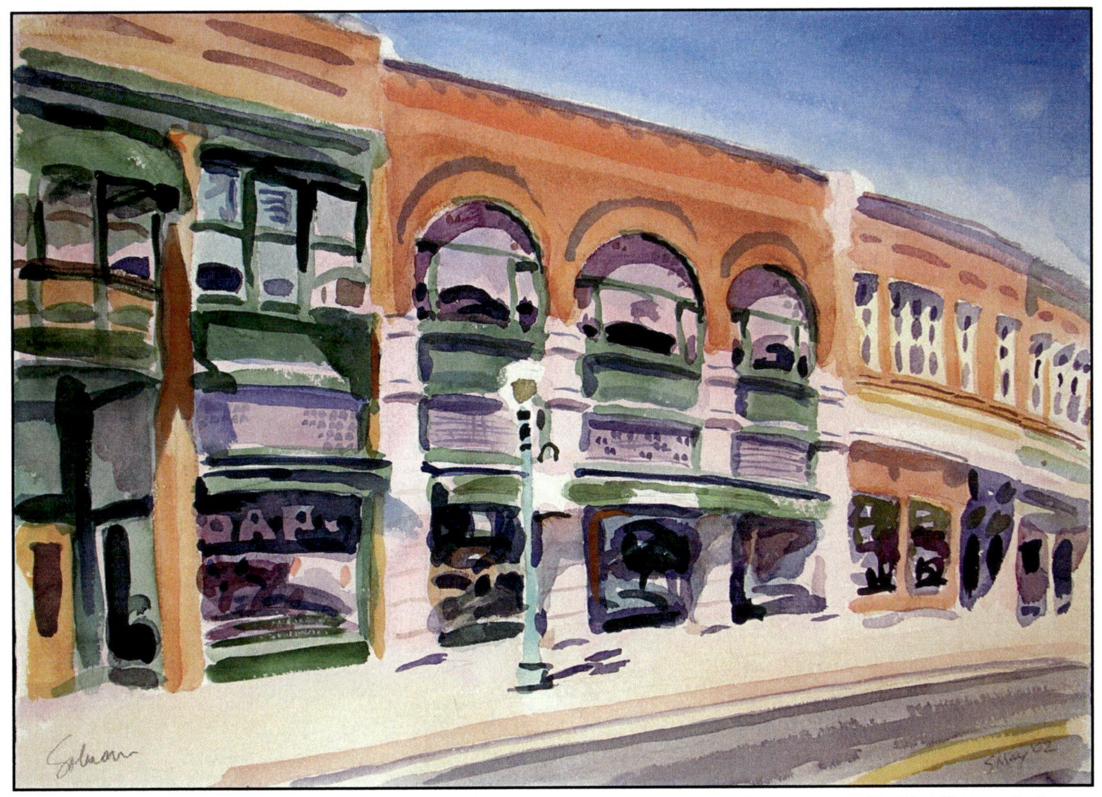

Common Grill, *Greg Sobran*

...terrible alarm clocks flying...

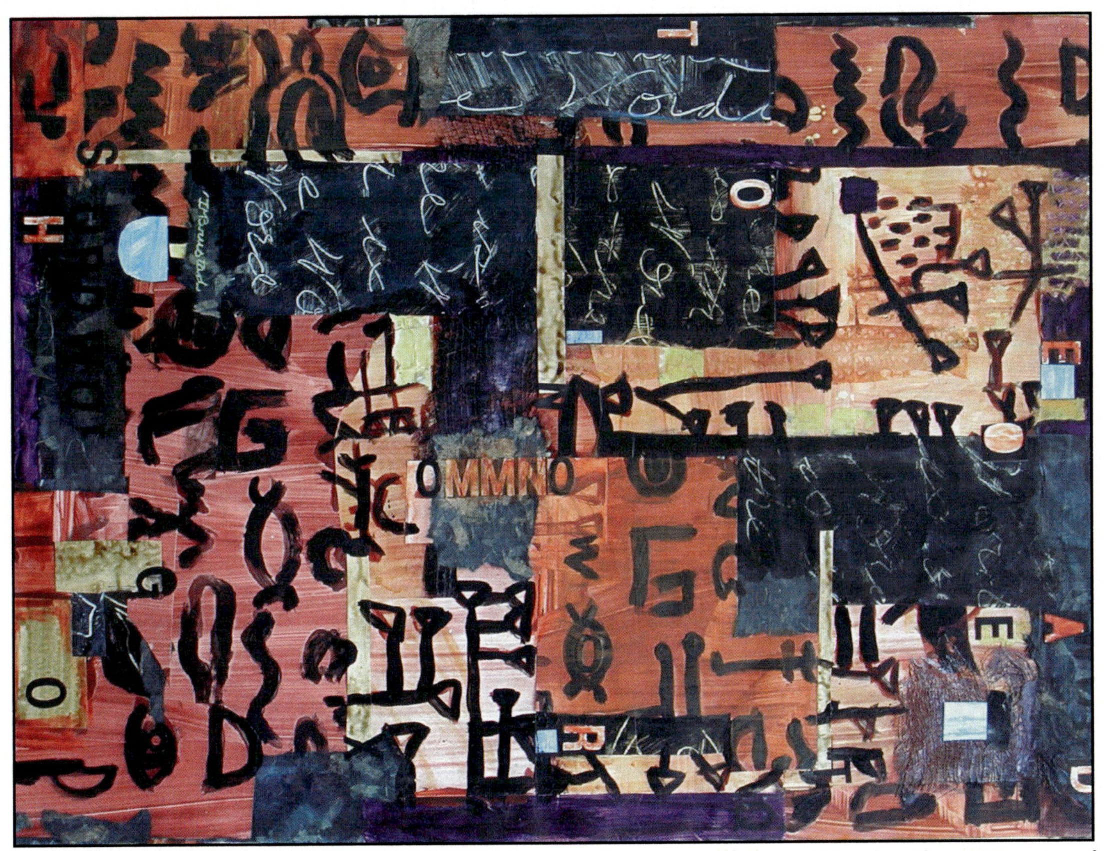

Words, *Ilona Brustard*

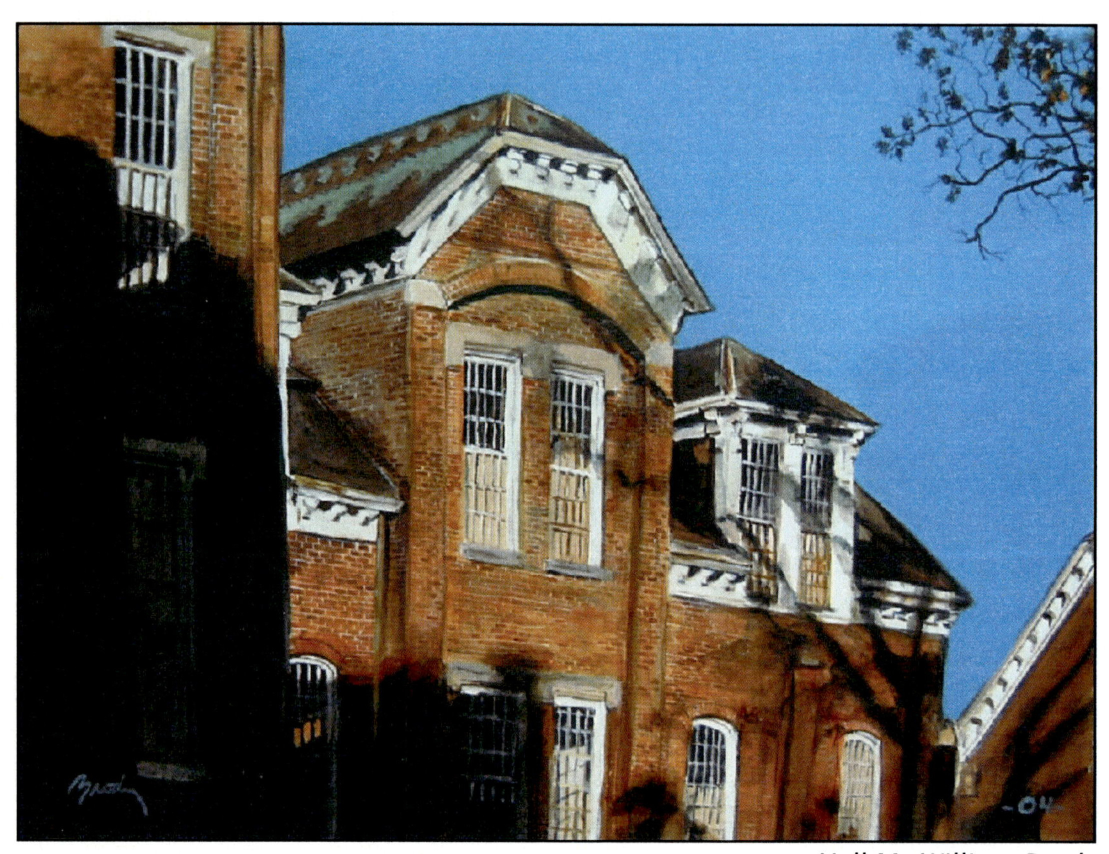

Hall M, *William Brody*

This Town

Would this town breathe without me?
Would traffic stop, streets fail to exist
without the map, the place
each street takes in my mind
the way its crosswalks, stop signs
intersect with memories I have
of yesterday. When I went running
in early morning, avoiding the spray
of underground sprinklers.

Would the church
still stand on the corner?
Without the lack of hours
minutes my images hold
when today seems further away
than the year I was 12 or 8, younger
asking how many more minutes
until the service was done
staring at kids in front of me.

Would train engines arrive
if I had forgotten
the direction to the railroad tracks?
Would people swim
in my neighbor's pool
if I had forgotten
how many footsteps it took to walk there
how to tell whether or not they were home
by looking into their garage.

Would I be sitting here
if the definition of this town
did not include me
or the sidewalk I sit on
the pond in front of me.
Would this town have the same name
without my image, touch, my hands
footprints, the paper I pick up
the things I leave behind.

Elizabeth J. Westrate

Subliminal Industrial Dreams

Boyhood home
backs up to a brake drum factory
the only plant in town

nighttime

windows open, metallic grease wafts in
presses
                mark time
subliminal industrial dreams.

Can't make it as a farmer?
drop an application at the plant
"Not Hiring" sign faded
sitting in the window too long

Can't sleep
look out the window at 1:30
midnight workers in a row-
        taking their lunch or dinner break?
sitting on crates
wavy, hazy, air behind them
        steamy plant atmosphere
        mid Michigan autumn night.

My family gave up on land years ago
don't even work in this town anymore

Our father
        once told us that before we were born
        our basement was
dug from the inside out
he and my uncles
hauled the dirt, bucket by bucket
up the stairs and through the wooden doors

and I thought
I'd like to have seen that.

Gregory Parker

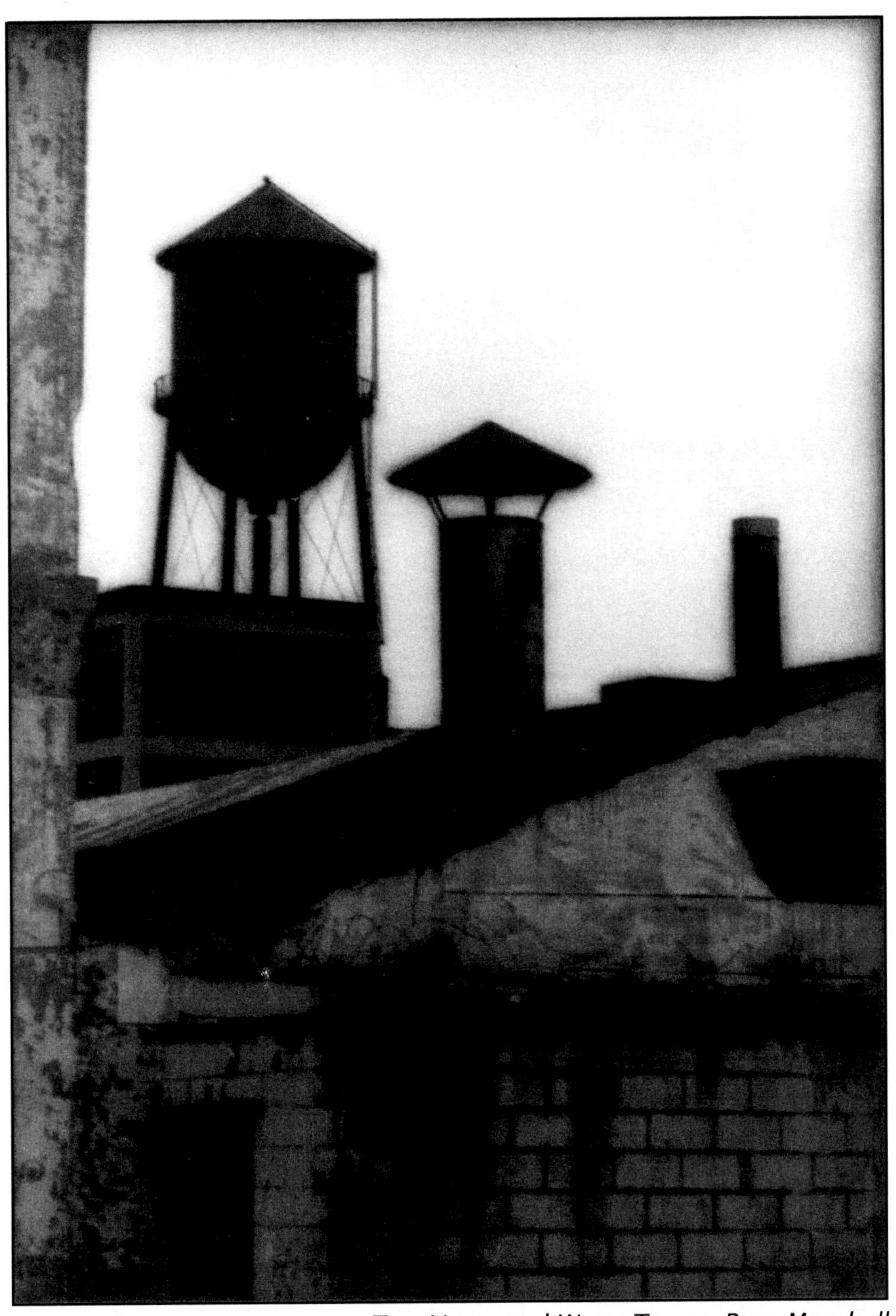

Two Vents and Water Tower, *Russ Marshall*

Blizzard at the Chelsea Fair

Too late I decide I would chase him through the gate, un-
strap him from that contraption
and pull him back,

but it's already begun,

the fans and the lights, the whole
thing rising
from its platform, and by god,
"She's a Brick House" being sung
sotto voce from the great beyond. Still

for a minute, watching
the rickety blur of their Blizzard
I would be the happiest woman in the world
if my son weren't in it.
Then

I catch a glimpse of him blur by
with what appears to be a smile—little
molecular smear
going somewhere, already been—but when

I try to wave at him I find
I'm frozen in time
by the notion of numbers, those

terrible alarm clocks flying
wildly around in the wind. I have

avoided disastrous statistics, those
alarm clocks scream, *until this minute.* More
than once, the shadow
of some enormous
machine has rolled right over me, but I
always walked away unscathed. While

children starved, I went
on diet after diet. Fish,
and bread, and cakes. God. The sloppy

temporary jobs I've done, the promises
broken blithely, the revealing
dress I once

wore to a wake. The devil

winks. He knows
I'm thinking, *Give me
back my boy and for whatever it's worth you can have my soul.*

"Mom," he says, touching

my shoulder when the whole thing's over, "there's
something on your skin."

I have yet to decide

if it's tears, or sweat, or just more skin
when he says, "Mom, I want to go again."

Laura Kasischke

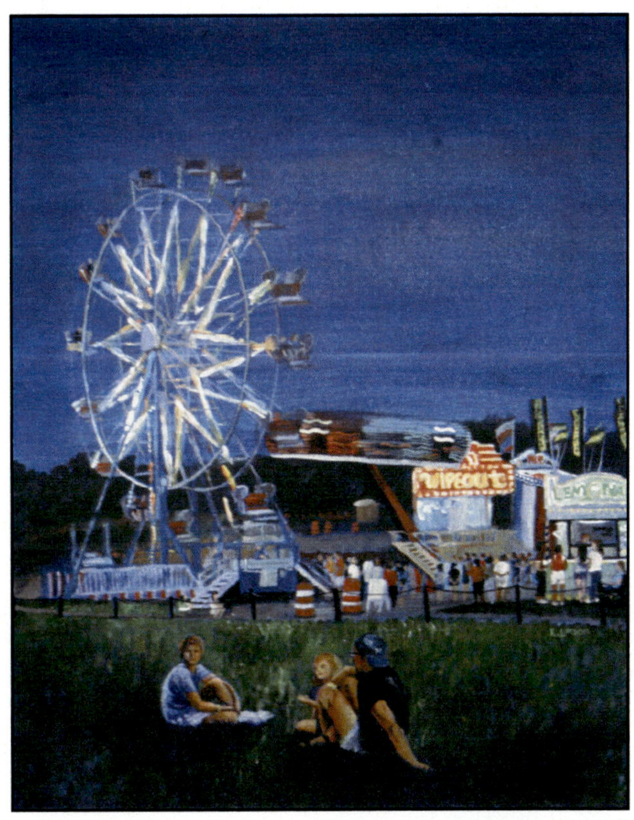

Untitled, *Katherine Larson*

Old Time Diner

The first concrete step
is several inches too high
takes an extra effort to climb.
The screen door slams shut
behind you, announcing you.

Red booths line the right wall
tables, small for four, large for two.
Stools at the bar counter
face a homemade pie display
coconut cream folds over
the side of its plate
an off-white version
of something grand.
The sound of food on the grill
fills in the conversation

In the morning
children order pancakes
in the shape of Mickey Mouse.
Men sit over black coffee
cream filled donuts
oatmeal with brown sugar and milk.
Farmers between animal feedings
retired men in the start of their day
discussing the excess of, or lack of water
in the muck fields at the edge of town
the local minister and his sermon last Sunday
the bill in the house or proposal A
the school board or road construction

At noon, the standard plate is served
hamburger and fries
warm silverware wrapped in napkins.
A tumbled glass of coke, mug of coffee
ten inch high glass of ice water.
The mix of dress represents the day
black suit and tie, cowboy boots
sundress, knee length skirts
diners stop to buy
a ten cent gumball
before leaving.

In the evening
Flo brings chocolate malteds
the taste of salt lingers on the edge
she leaves the extra
in its mixer tin on the table.
And ice cream sundaes with two cherries
brought from behind the alley
that serves as a kitchen.

The staff cleans up for the night
preparing for tomorrow
filling cups and saucers
miniature pitchers of cream
selections of jams and jellies
sugar in small town versions
of a column or vase.

Elizabeth J. Westrate

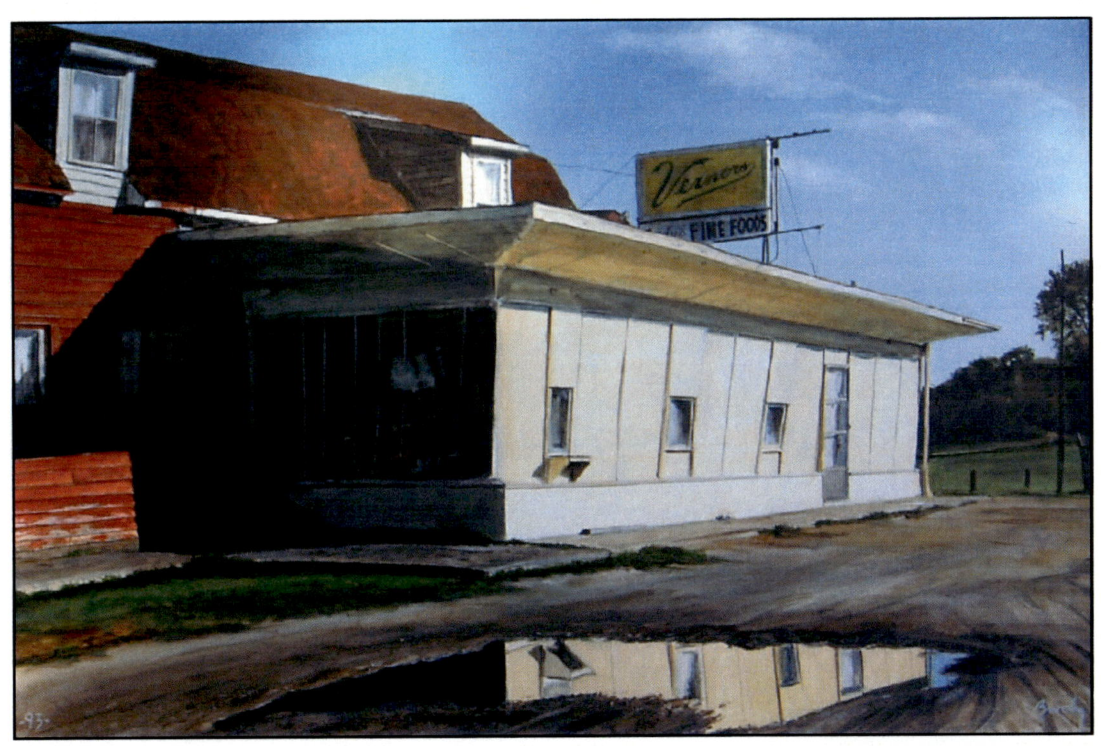

Diner, *William Brody*

11 Sighs at Zou Zou's Café

Truant clouds exhale sweet shadows,
tint store fronts with the past—
bay windows yearn for 19th Century,
café au lait/espresso fade into
oats, 19 cents a bushel.

Nymph in knee-socks
slouched over biology book
ferries me back onto a stool
at McIroy's soda shop in 1968,
perfume is stronger than coffee.

Businessmen whisper
through their mustaches,
rub clammy palms over
worried knuckles,
cappuccino makes them flush.

Mayans nibbled on coffee beans
shimmering until Conquistadors sacked
Yucatan and exported the euphoria—
getting high isn't what it used to be.

Man at window with laptop types
equation for a lost conscience—
has forgotten history is always personal.

Expresso machine whines in tune
with girl's track team's hoots and hollers—
burning bras still light up the night!

Some of us write love letters, some
write novels, and still others write
letters of foreclosure—not everyone
who gets the calling answers.

Cashier looks like an old girlfriend,
thick black eyebrows and Syrian chin—
I am the one who grew old.

Dark chocolate and coffee, good
for the heart, reads a sticker taped
to the napkin holder—cut a vein
and see what comes out.

Latte to go, please—
football and piano practice,
driveway full of potholes,
this weather can't last.

Cell phone's operatic howl,
"Hurry home," she says, "To
see the northern lights"—
no more broken promises.

Doug Smith

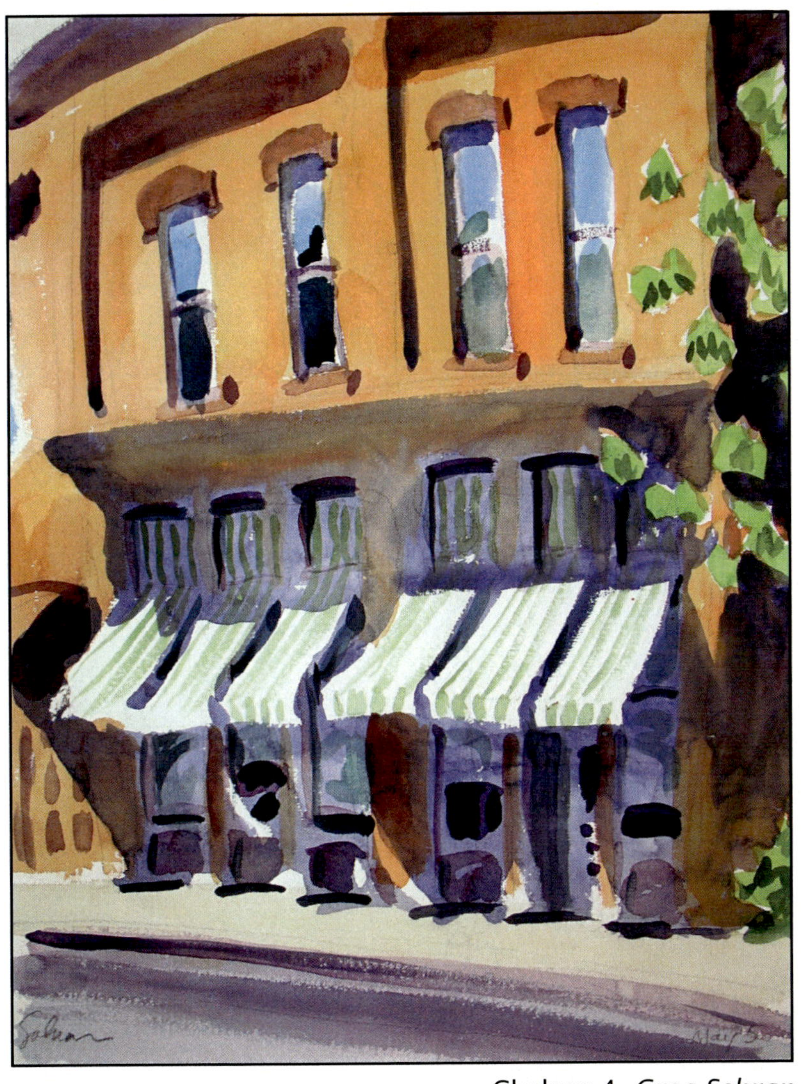

Chelsea 4, *Greg Sobran*

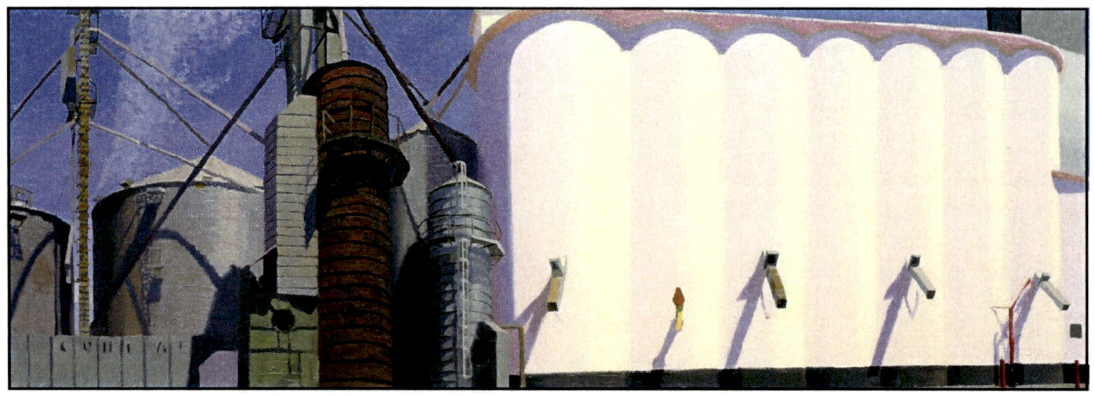

The Big H, *Elaine Wilson*

Village without a River

Morning
Blind milky-white caterpillars rise over
the village along the railroad tracks, tranquil
giants dozing in alabaster cocoons.
Twenty-seven elevated grain silos joined
together, molting in the early morning sunlight.
What a comfort they are, pedaling his bicycle
up Main Street.

Surfacing from the morning mist, dressed
in a pale pink sleeveless blouse, long legs
gleam between white ankle sox and shorts.
Feet glide like just sharpened skates on
January ice over the asphalt on Wilkinson St.
Her long brown hair swooshes ecstatic—
from a block away she could be mistaken
for her granddaughter, the ballerina.
He imagines the woman is Ruth of Judah,
secretly emigrated from an ancient grave,
here to quietly inspire a sense of grace
in the common errand.

Large men sit before Formica tables at
Pierce's Pastries, assessing the daily news
in between sips from small cups filled with
hazelnut decaf. Polite discussion on why
General Patton wasn't allowed to liberate
Berlin sinks into a more injurious row.

Choruses of uh-huhs, yeah-buddys, and
low belly laughs detonate in the air like a
small scale artillery barrage entertaining
the younger patrons with the sound and
smell of leisure earned. He winces at
the self-importance, but longs to join them.

Afternoon
Another day displacing topsoil, making a refugee
of the earth at the corner where Darius Pierce
planted corn one-hundred seventy years ago,
the high pitched whine of the bulldozer finally
drowned out by the mad screams of four cranes
flying low over the new CVS construction site.
The backhoe rocks onto its haunches, thrusts
a shovel into the dusty sky as the cranes fly east
toward the wetland behind the elementary school
where he takes Saturday walks with his children.
Grim clouds conspire, cover the horizon in a thick
pea green soup, expel the sun with a whip
of screaming white light, turn rain into stones
falling in a hail of sin, pelt his face and cut
the legs out from under him. He crawls along
the ground looking for the feet of Mary Magdalene
to lead him from this Mount of Olives, remembers
what a holy man told him in a crowded Ann Arbor
room on a cold winter night—
"Even the most horrible can be redeemed."

Was this once a corn field, or maybe an Indian
burial ground? All lush and green today, thinks
a father, eyes blinking, trying to focus on the drama
before him.   Sons and daughters practice foot work,
listen to their coach holler out plays, willing the ball
up field to a forward with the best chance of kicking
the sphere in the net. Hyena giggles and dangling
epithets skip along the grass like pebbles across
a still lake in summer. The crackle & wheeze of air
pushing water from a plastic bottle, the thick thud
of a child tripped to the ground inspires a familiar ache.
The sun splits a cloud, casts a narrow shadow
over Papo field, separates forwards from wingbacks,
fathers from sons, winners from losers—the ones
who can imagine a future from the ones who don't.

Dusk
No Hunters/No Trespassers, reads the sign
nailed to a leafless poplar. A jogger mumbles
outrage, trots along dirt road leading out of town
past the Methodist Home. "What do they want,
these tourists who move to our untilled fields
from the great metropolis—turn the countryside
into one continuous suburb from Dearborn
to Chicago?" Gravel squirts loose from
under his new running shoes, footing unstable
after weeks with no rain. The jogger straightens
his gait, his strides become more deliberate.
"Tie your dog up? Stop shooting the deer?
Keep your cats away from my bird feeder!"
He closes his eyes, sees a young man passing
the hat for a revolution that won't be televised,
hears the muffled roar of 'the last poets' fade.
"You're either part of the solution or...." He left
Detroit because his tears had turned to vinegar
weeping for the drunks who slept on his lawn
hot summer nights, their heads lying in the high
grass, feet stretched across the sidewalk, so
peaceful until the grumbling from their empty
stomachs awoke them. This is what he tells
himself when the shame of never having invited
a weary drunk to crash on the couch becomes
too much, the nagging doubt that a wino asleep
on the grass could have been the one foretold
in Hebrews, the stranger everyone is waiting for?
The jogger dashes down the road, thinking about
a fallen Brahmin, praying the first step toward
grace is just beyond that cluster of trees,
if only he can quiet his mind, run fast enough
to reach the crest of the hill in time to catch the sun.

Night
One hundred and twenty feet of red masonry
and limestone, a tower with four clock faces
keeps vigil over his village without a river.
Flemish refugees gave locals the recipe. Shale
scooped up from pits left by continental glaciers,
crushed, mixed, and molded—cobalt and ash
added for color—baked in a kiln over a bed of coke.
Back breaking work pitching bricks, two and three

in each hand, up to the catcher who wore the soles
of used leather shoes over his hands to prevent
blisters and broken knuckles. Pulleys lifting
balance wheels, pendulums, counter-weights,
tension cables, forests of scaffolding supporting
the dream of collective time. For years the clock
was wound by hand, two men cranking
an enormous spring every week, their fingers
gnarled up like hickory branches. Today only
the surface of history is kept, a replication of time.
Twelve hundred-pound bells announce the hour.
Manure and lilac dampen the air. Westminster
chimes pleasantly dull. Dirt, cool in his hands,
kneeling in the garden under the olive tree,
waiting for the Romans.

Doug Smith

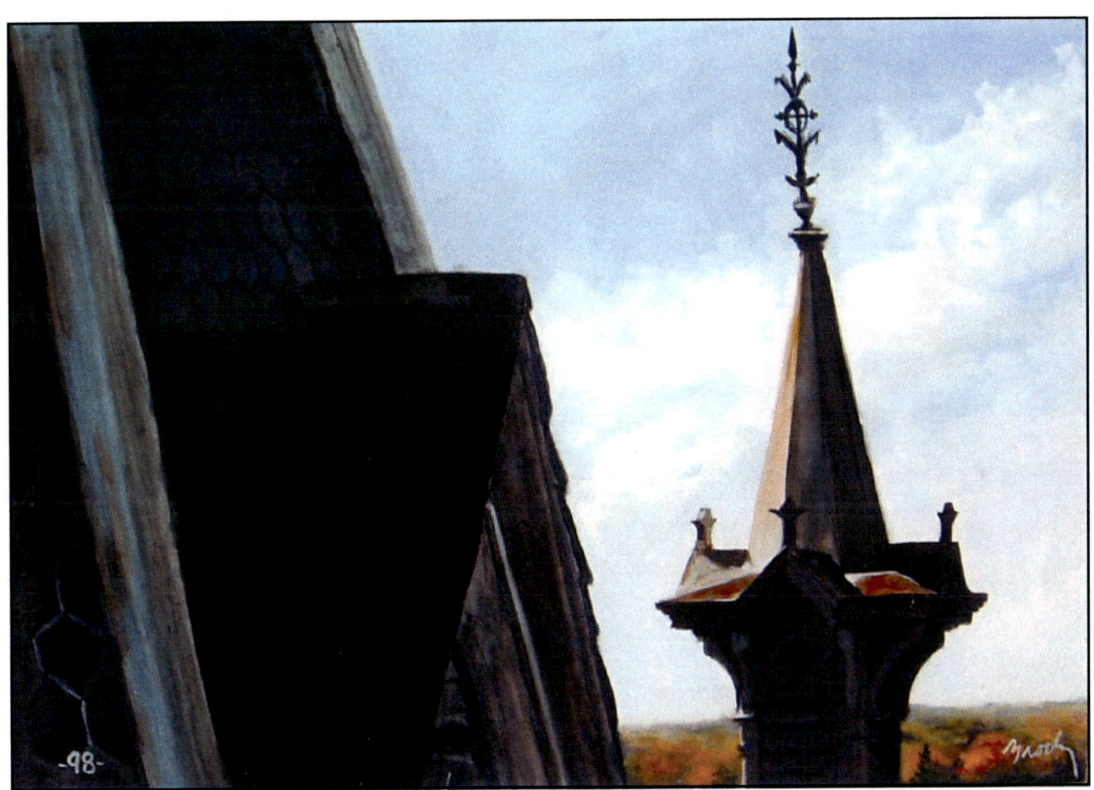

Steeple Tower, *William Brody*

...a buzzing fist of gold...

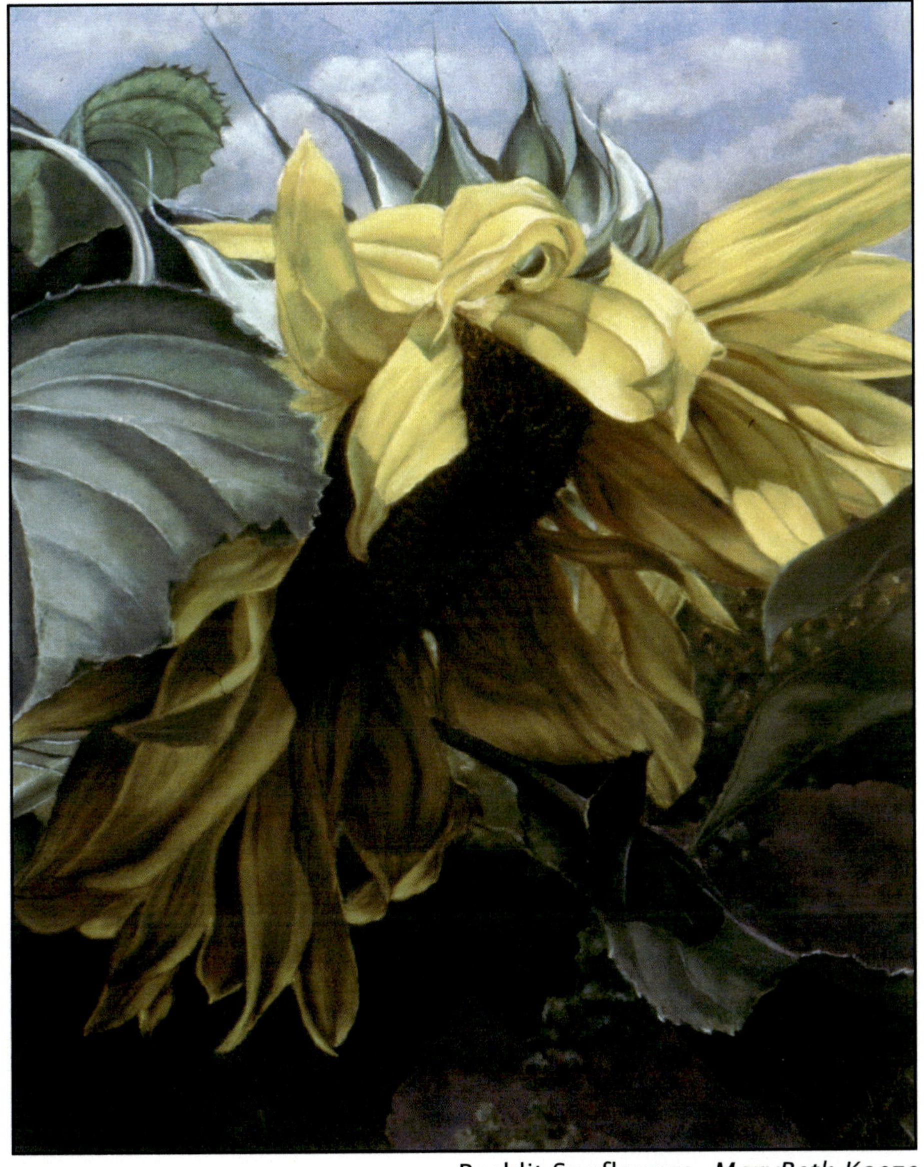

Backlit Sunflowers, *MaryBeth Koeze*

From My Father's Garden
"Transplant on cloudy days, Susie." Harold W. Croisant

My shovel sucked the mud
Out of the rain puddle
Under the eave above
The kitchen window
Of my new house
In my new home town.
I turned the pot upside down
And pulled out lilies
Of the valley from
Below the eave beside
The kitchen door where
I used to park my bike,
A brand new shiny two wheeler,
All my own, never been ridden
By brother, sister, or cousin.
Into the soupy mess I planted
The green sprigs that promised
White bells of seventh grade perfume,
Smells rumored to be toxic.
On higher ground
In partial shade
I troweled several small
Holes through the mulch
For the three part purple faces
And green hearts of the
Hope that grew for my grandmother
To see through the glass
From her bed where she lay
Useless except for
Loving me so surely
That I could believe in God.

I broke apart the tangled clumps
Of tough and bulbous day lily roots
That first had come from Aunt Faith's,
The homestead where she raised
Three sons of her sister
Who braved the Colorado wilderness
Without a man
But couldn't beat the cancer in her brain.
These roots sprout three-foot tall
Stems of triple layered embarrassments

76

Of orange.
I've grown them before
In my rose garden by the sea
Where they mocked my hydrangeas
And invaded the lawn.
Here, back in their Michigan home,
I'll spread them
Everywhere
Where everyone can see
The glory
Of my father's garden.

Catherine Croisant Varner

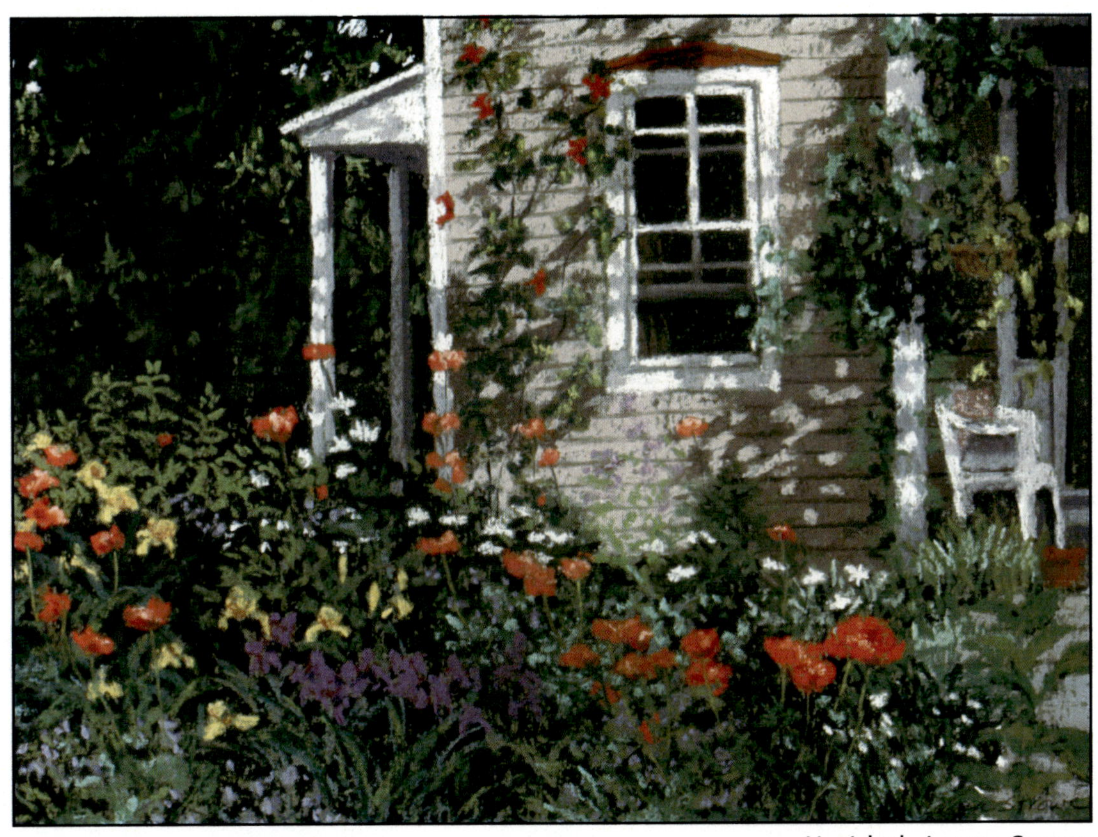

Untitled, *Laura Strowe*

Bellwether

In line at Polly's Market

He comes up to my elbow
Smells sweetly of animal waste
And diesel fuel, ageless beyond sixty
After staring ahead for a time
He swivels around slowly
Scans me with gem-sharp eyes, says

"They just cut the sweet corn.
Summer's over. Wheat too…
Up 52 'fore Stockbridge.
It's over. Summer."

He grins for the ages, pays
In quarters and balled-up singles
Walks out into the parking lot
Under a waning, umber moon.

David B Sing

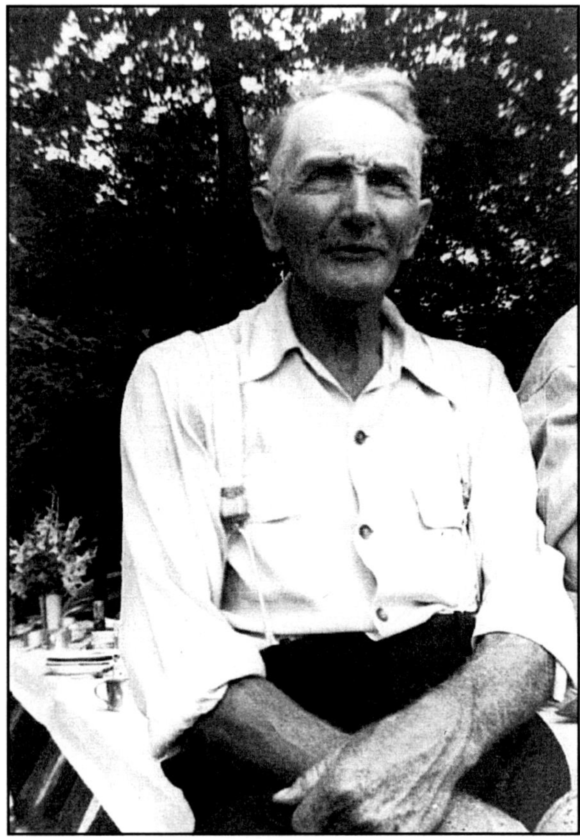

CC Dowling, *Mildred Dowling Clark*

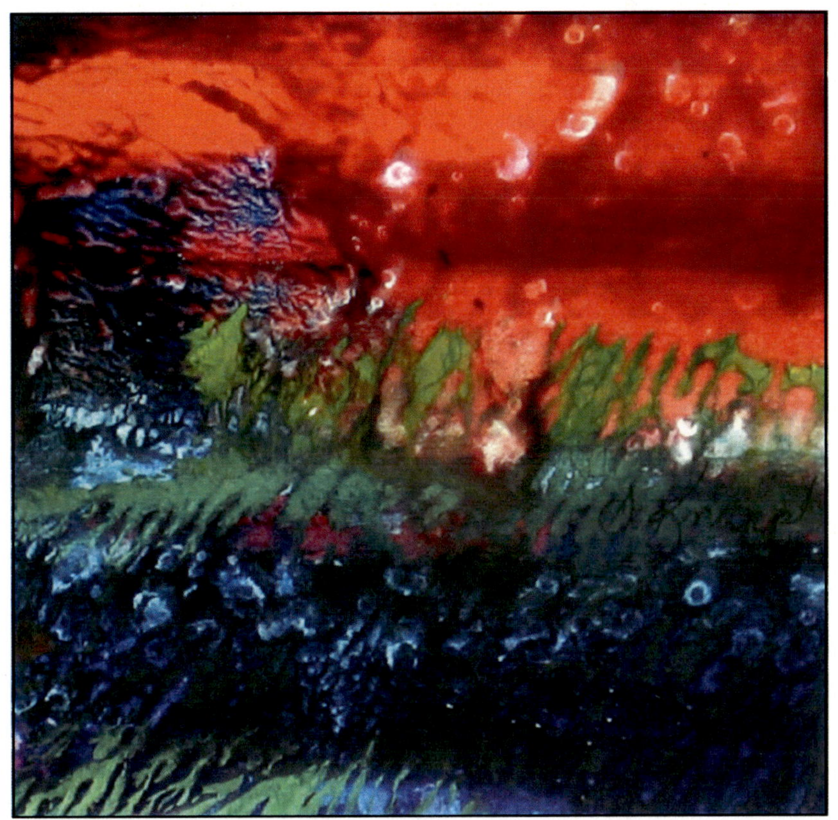

October Sky, *Sandy Knapp*

Microeconomics

Up on the hill, the farm
is swallowed by the gravel pit.
Orchards yield to houses.
In the courthouse,
selectmen hear
the developer's pitch:
every citizen has a stake.
By the creek at the edge
of the township
where the paper mill
once stood, cottonwoods
turn over their hands:
silver and green, silver and green.

Judith Kerman

Clothes on the line

Clothes I've hung on the line
        flap a mantra,
                sending prayers on rhythmic,
                        ragged strips of cloth.

Thus are my dreams flung about,
        haphazardly.

You fret at the disorder strung across your lawn,
fear to lose your head.

Watch where you're going,
learn to duck.

Clothes on the Line Reprise

        Clothes on the line
                flap a mantra
                        prayers of rhythmic
                                beating strips of thought.
                        Dreams fly about
                joyfully

Hermione Miles Gorney

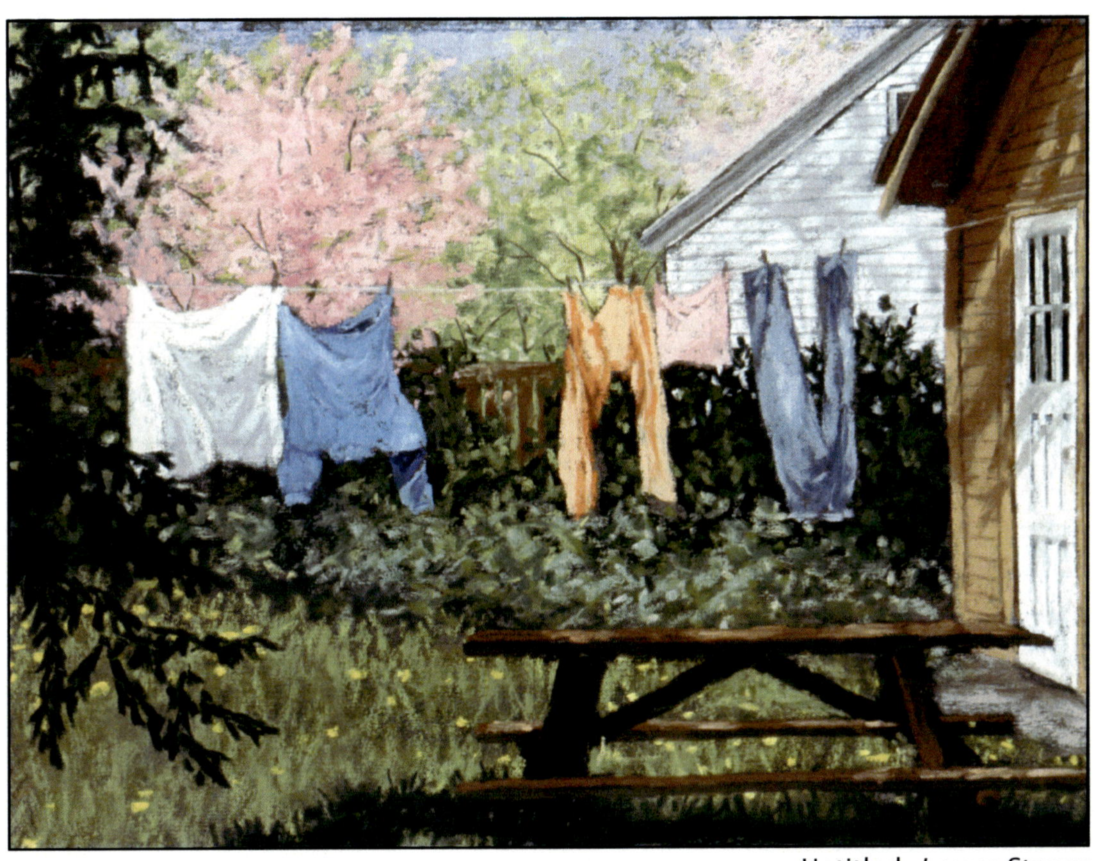

Untitled, *Laura Strowe*

Chain-link Fence

I can tell a green field from
a cold steel rail.

Rectangled earth
    strung a thousand times a
        thousand-thousand meters.
Galvanized metalica
    linked and knitted
        ribboned wire diamond webs.
Height, three feet; length eight.
    Feign to confine, enclose, impound,
        compound ownership.
Rusting broken forged perimeters
    cheaply marking exclusive
        private right to use.
Caging barking dogs
        keeping out meanderers
        excluding curiosity, exploration.
Steel symbols segregating
    lawns, yards, schools, prisons, malls,
        office blocks, beaches, parking lots.
Cornering the last irregularities of
    receding wilderness
        in chained reaction.

Will the world make more sense
with another fifty feet of
chain-link fence?

Kent Ashton Walton

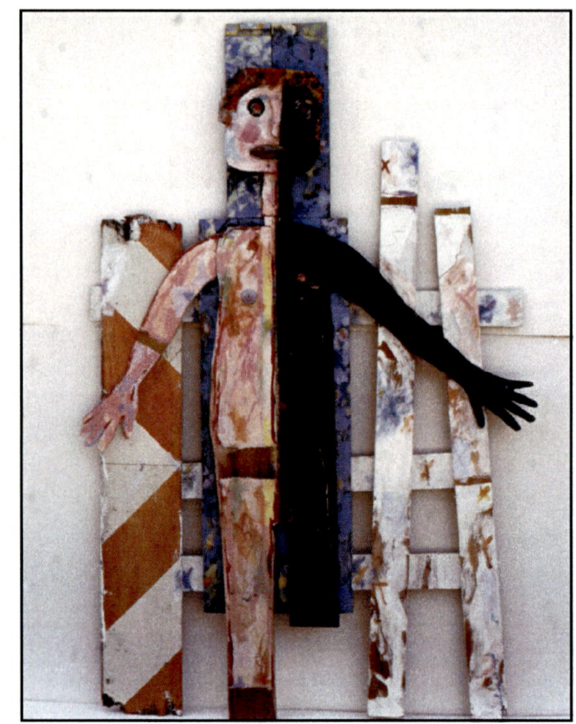

Fence Boy, *Joan Painter Jones*

82

Contradiction

We want the woods, just not too close, set up a perimeter of manageability
Wildlife just not too wild, the wolf lost in memory of others
Tame deer are stalked across flat land satisfying incorrigibility
Dirt roads are paved so that SUV's can drive them, soccer dads and mothers.

We want a good grocery store, a better video store, a closer ice rink
Instantaneous gratification through senseless traveling
We don't have a traffic problem, we are a traffic problem, think
Distance doesn't reduce time, if you build it we will come often, denying.

There is no more corn on the roads, instead trails of fast food detritus mark travel
The coyote song is sad, bordering on the periphery of waking thought and sleep
Shadow at our margins, that they remain a product of our waste and nature's marvel
Issues that seem trivial in the moment mount to catastrophic consequences for all
to reap.

Oscar Marx

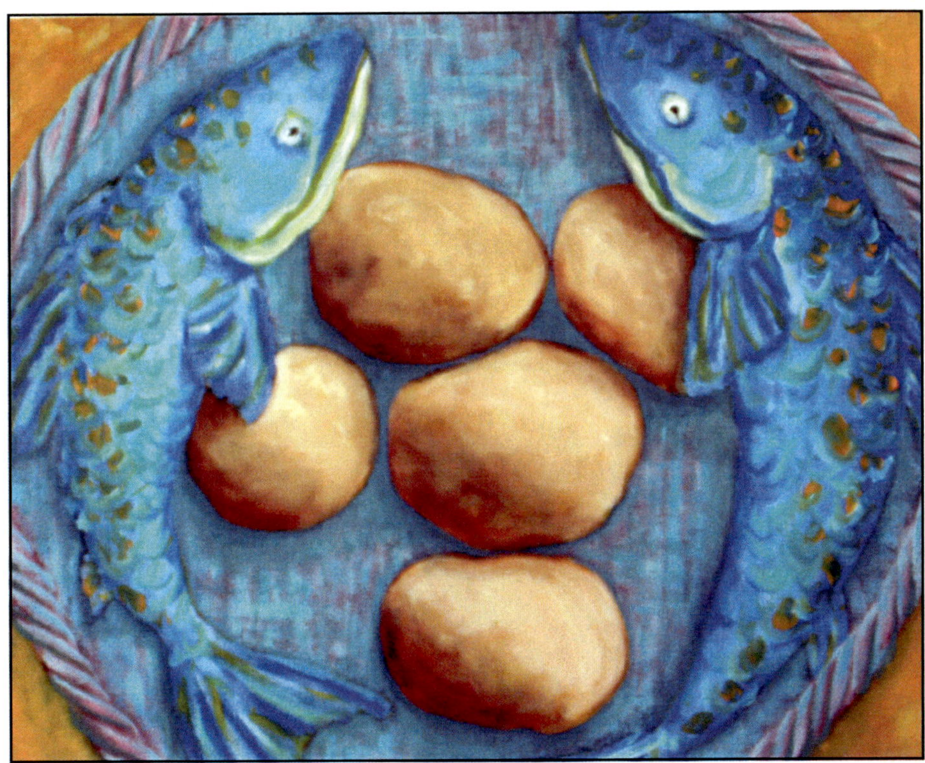

Loaves and Fishes, *Heidi Kraepel*

...nectar spills from our mouths...

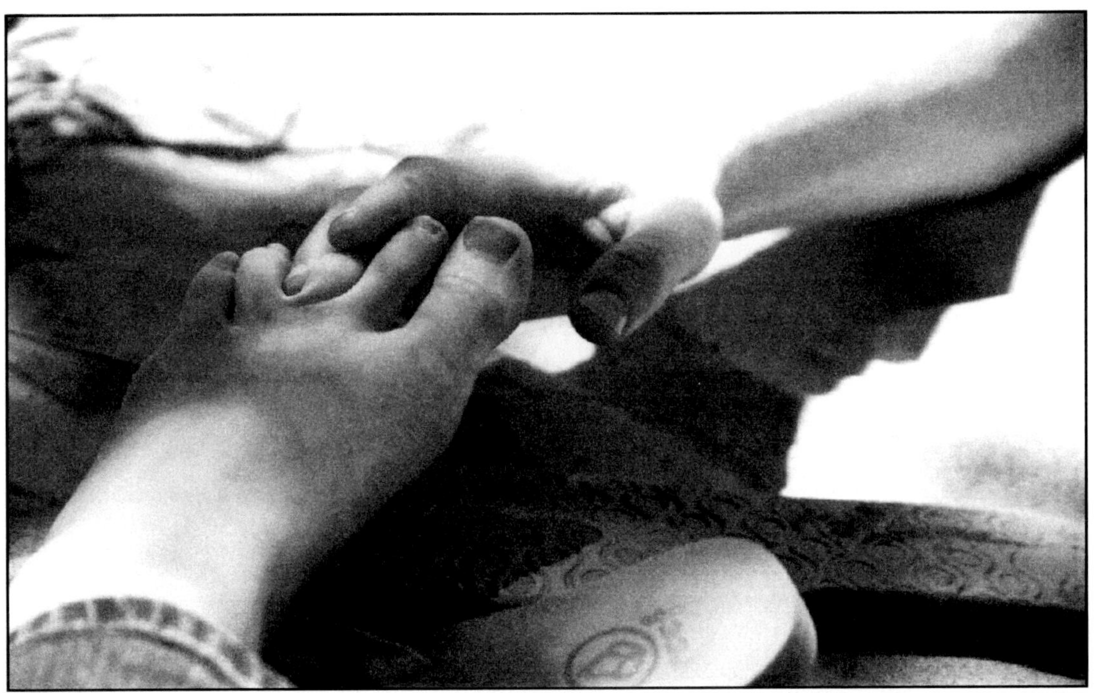

The Footgrab, *Alexandra Tinsley*

(Untitled #1)

Every time I move my lips
I kiss your body
When I drink my coffee
I am kissing your mouth
When I talk I am kissing
Your neck
When I breathe softly
I am kissing your belly
When I eat
I kiss your thighs
Your body is my
Sustenance
And even when
We are apart
I feed on
You.

Melody Vassoff

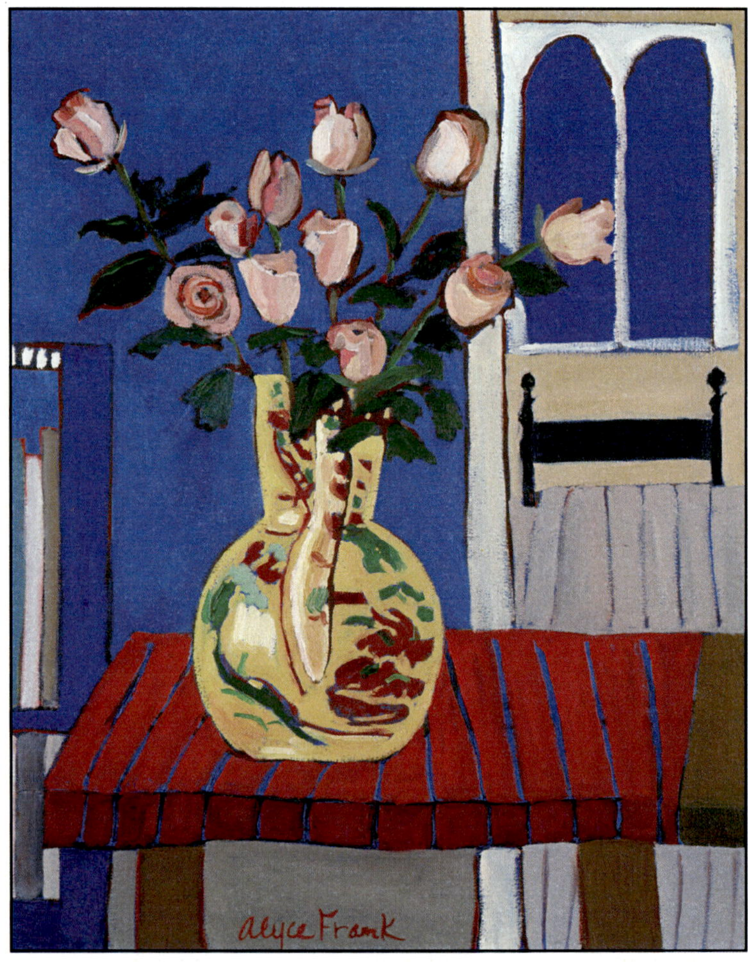

Roses on a Table, *Alyce Frank*

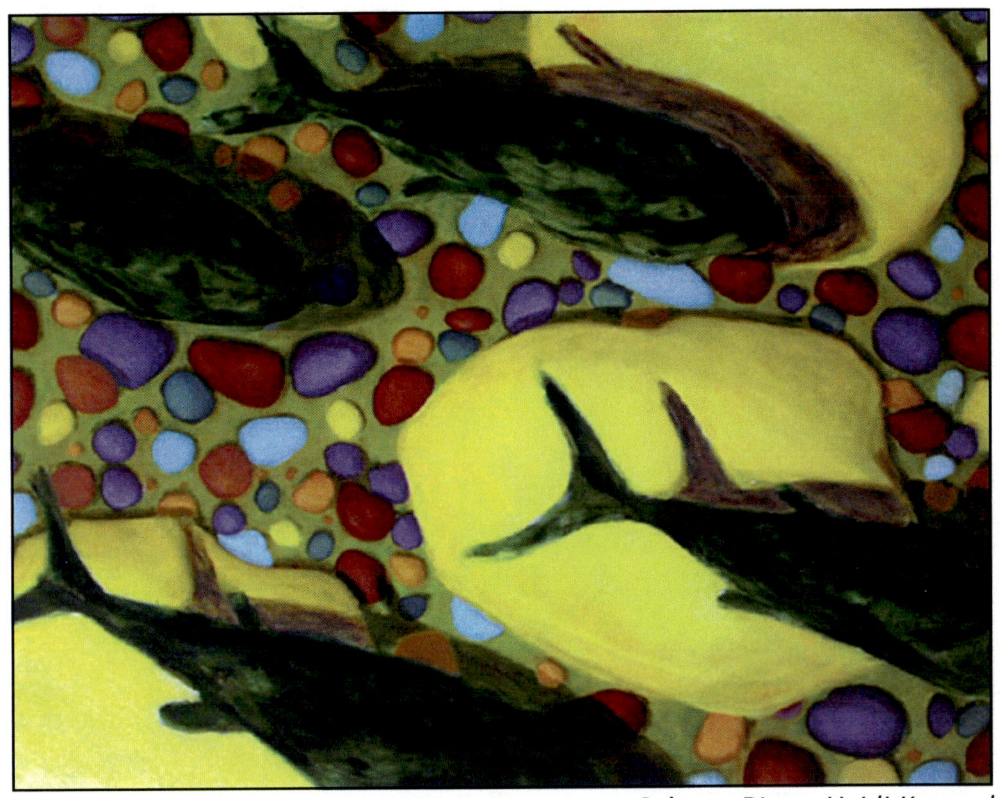

Salmon River, *Heidi Kraepel*

Burn

That fire,
of all fires
burns so
bright and deep
it flares
white-hot
leaving
the embers
to smolder
in my belly
until all
I can smell
is
seared
flesh.

Melody Vassoff

(Untitled #2)

She lies there on the sweat–soaked
sheets
feeling exactly like a half-crushed
cigarette
guttering out in the snow
And as surely as the smoke
dissipates
she feels her soul
leaving on the cold, damp
wind

Melody Vassoff

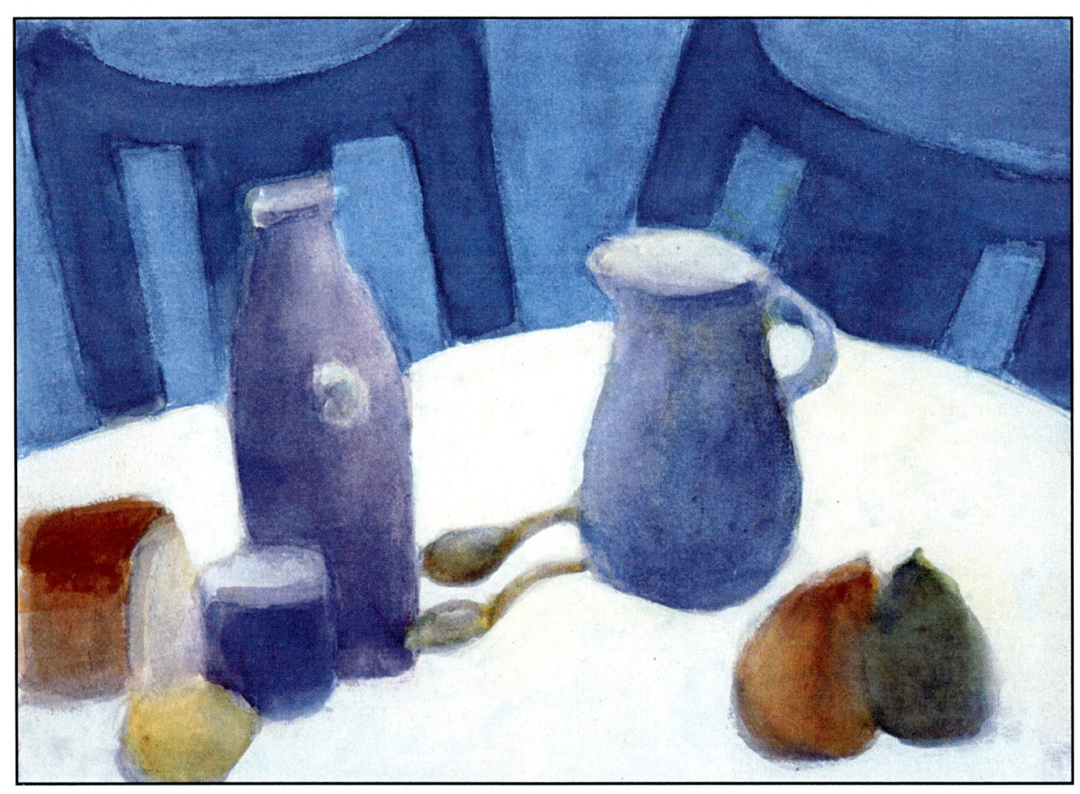

Early Morning, *Madeleine Vallier*

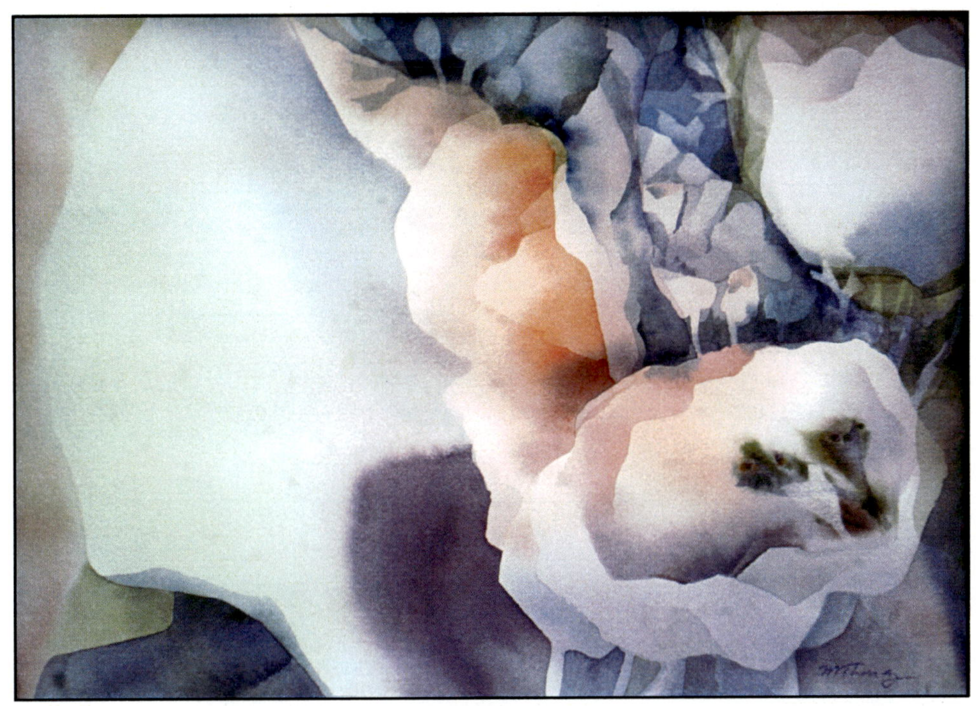

Dreamlike Shell of the Past, *Monette Thorrez*

Spring

Demeter
If you are
To give birth
Do so
On
My watch
I want to
Swim upwards
Through the
Slippery
Birthwater
Searching
For light
And air
As the
Sun
Makes its
Return

Melody Vassoff

Peach

Sitting on a bench at rest with you,
I share a very ripe peach,
start to cut it in half. The juice
Runs and drips beyond my control.

Abandoning correctness, I eat my share
And pass to you with sticky hands.
We laugh.
Nectar spills from our smiling mouths.

Life tastes sweet, smells like heaven,
Doesn't come in bite-sized pieces.

Hermione Miles Gorney

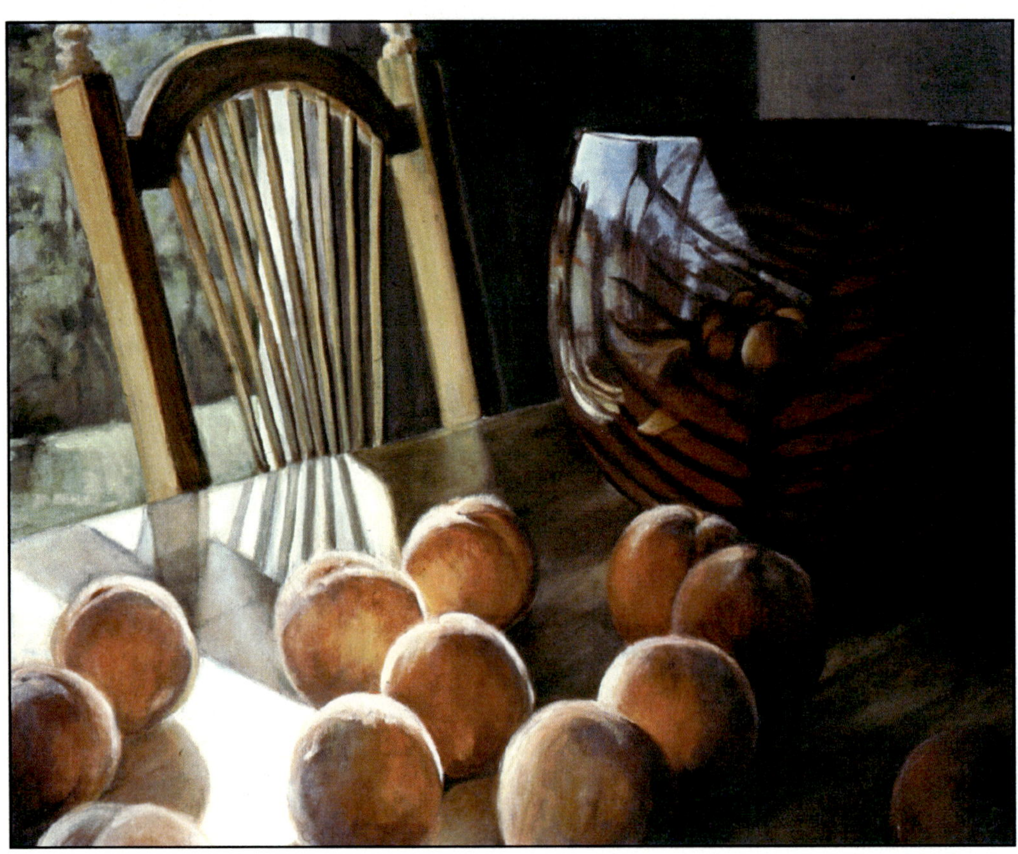

Ripening, *MaryBeth Koeze*

...raining yellow daggers...

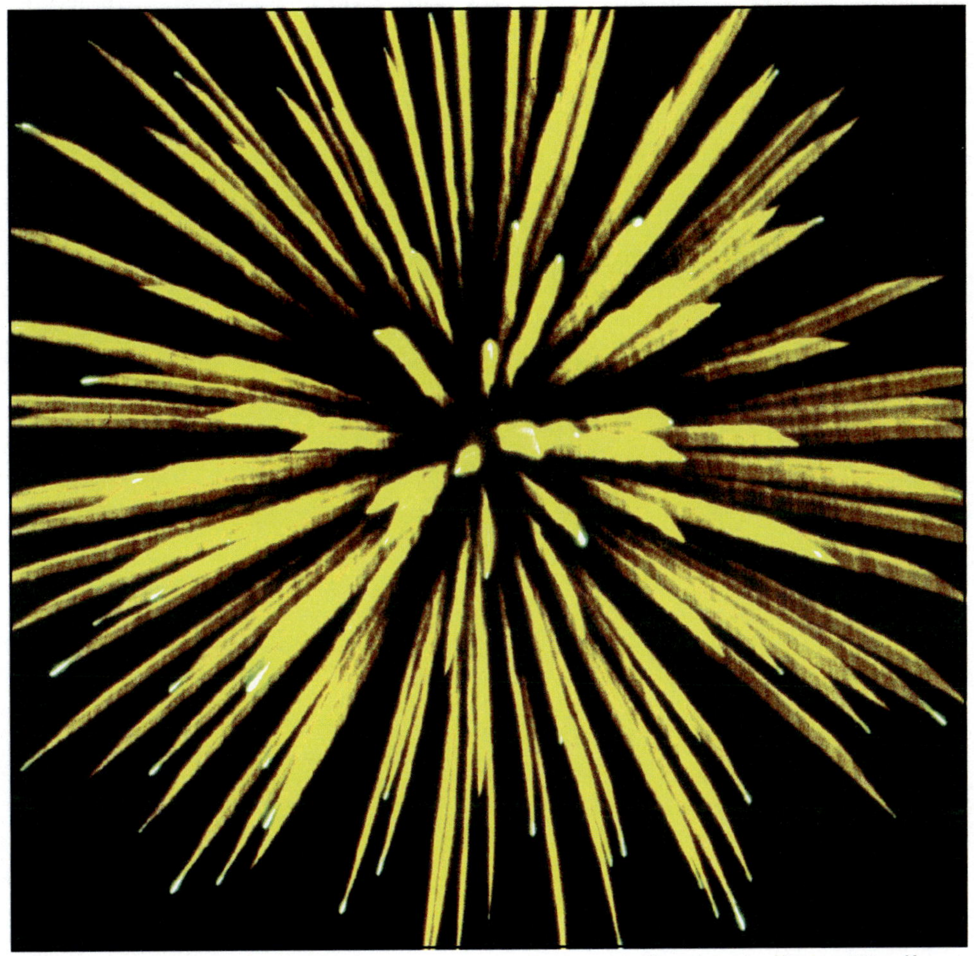

Sunburst, *Stan Woollams*

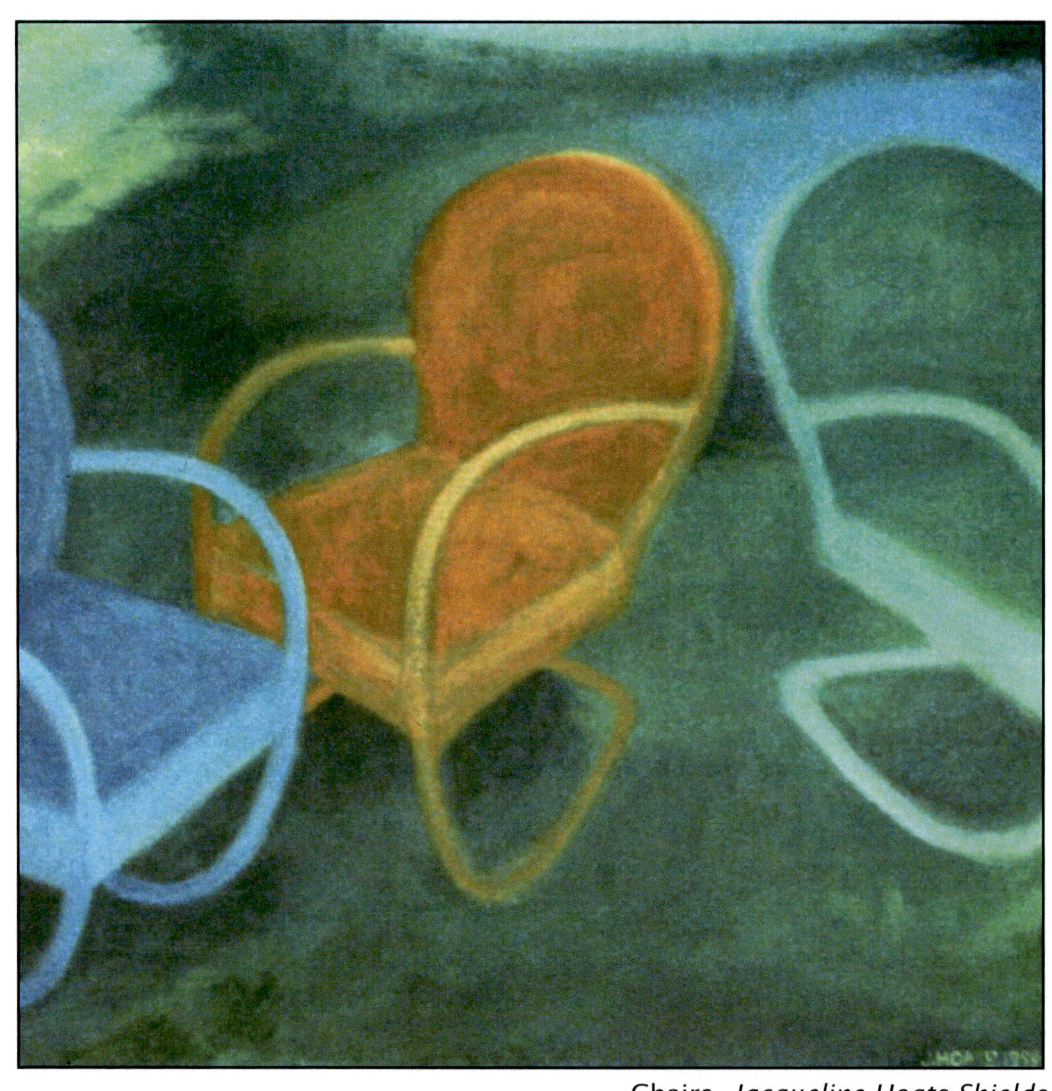

Chairs, *Jacqueline Hoats Shields*

Out of the Garden

The bees are the first to notice
how cold air creeps out of the swamp
how yesterday's sweet taste is now dull
how the cosmos droop under the weight of the rain.

They choose more carefully now
nestle their bodies, warm them against
delightful golden petals
suck the juices from warm, fragrant bosoms.

I walk out of the garden and
into the house. May hands are full
of flower smells, basil smells, dirt
smells. I gaze into the silvered mirror
as I wash the morning
off my hands. Some new gray
hairs, more liver spots, more flesh
beneath my chin.

And I wonder, as I never did in April:
will you still love me
as my hair turns to straw
as my breasts sink to the earth
when my teeth sit in a pink plastic cup
  on the edge of the sink?

Rosemary Caruso

Eggs and Toast

She makes me toast and boiled eggs
and we talk about the plumbing

I hold my breath and strain to knot my laces,
bending forward, struggling with the frayed ends
in the eyelets

Catching a glimpse of an exposed knee
peeking from the folds of her robe
my gaze continues upward to meet her eyes

But they focus on the clock
ticking towards the work day
and when she returns my stare
I'm tying the other shoe.

Gregory Parker

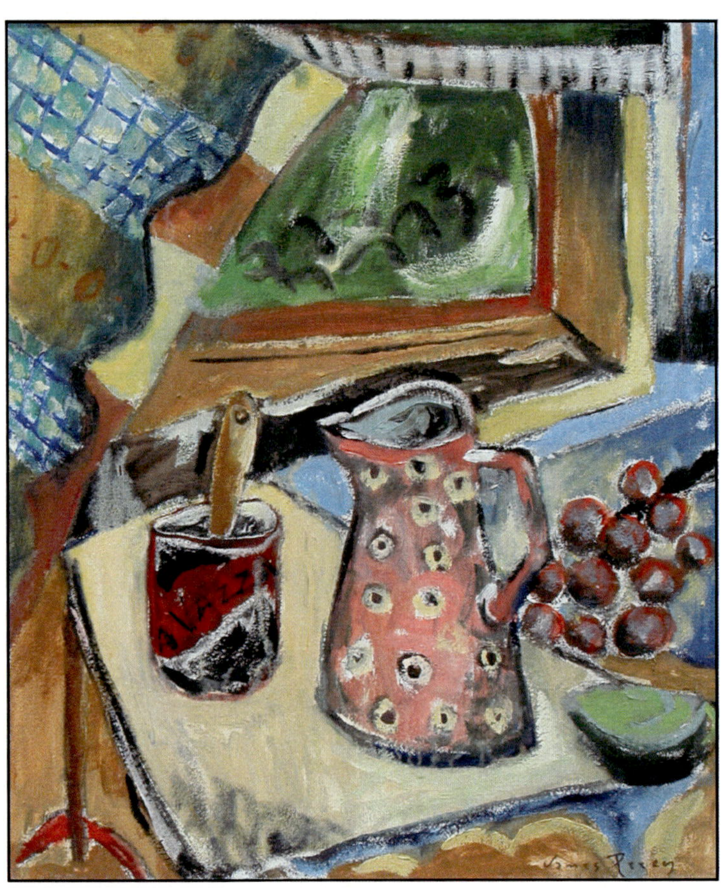

Still Life with Coffeepot, *James Peery*

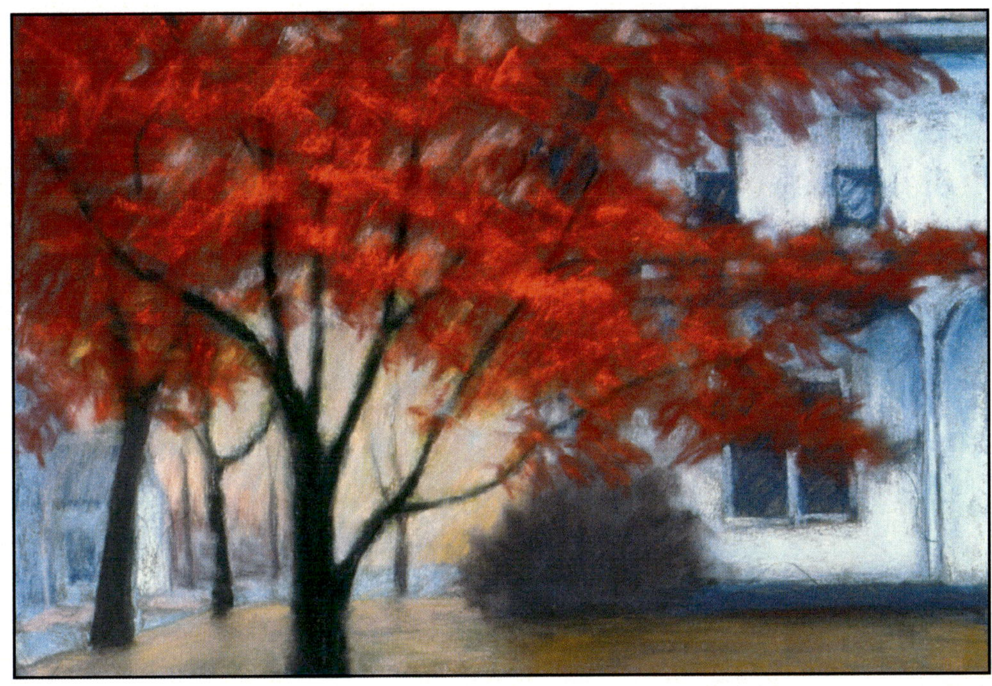

The Red Tree, *Teresa Freed*

Stained Glass

At a landing on our stairs
ladybugs gather in the
recesses
of a stained glass window
that filters warm, colored rays
into our house when the sun rises.

Sometimes I stop on the landing,
where the window is eye level
and I look out,
deciphering the landscape through the wavy
tinted glass.

When I squint
I can make out the neighbor's house,
or the asphalt shingles on the roof below
or maybe oaks in the backyard
and the kids from next door
running
with their golden dog.

Gregory Parker

Local Legend

This morning the awful surprise of a dead
greyhound in lilies *silver*
on silver and hollow. The sky
goes wild with laughter

and the seeds of doubt sprout small bald
shoots in ground and glimmer, like
rosary beads in the hands
of our local legend Sister

Henry-Anne who claimed they turned
from glass to gold one day at mass. But we
knew they never did. Sister
Henry-Anne was lonely

and getting old, and she wanted
her name in the paper the way
some of us want to be held and
are perfectly willing to spin

straw into fool's gold for it. And anyway we knew
the last real miracle here was when
Catholic Central slaughtered Rockford
42 to 10. There

was blood in the parking lot then. Glass
shattered and sparkled
like white eels on the church lawn. Toilet paper strung
umbilical cords through trees, streaming

wet by morning
and white as ghouls against
a purple October sky. They say
two pom-pom girls in the Catholic cemetery

took on the whole team
themselves that night. There was
the cold-sweat of marble
in the air, stale
green carnations, the earth-
kiss of mulch in wild hair. I know
I was there. *Heed*
a warning the horoscope in the local paper

almost never says, and
that may be because
Linda Lovelace is the only
true star this town

has ever had. And Tuesday
is usually
the tepid day of death, though today
it's just this empty

boat of a silver dog, thumped
with a buzzing
fist of gold: Bees
have attached a hive to its spine, and they drone

in and out of it like
a handbag stuffed
with gossip and honey, and another
story that goes-

In 1967
a wagonload of angry
clowns passed though this town, and all
the Catholic girls stepped out

in night-frost and no clothes. Though
the Shriners still deny it, that
procession lasted for nights. And I
say, who's to say a clown

however bitter
however old
couldn't sire a human child among us
like a god? *Here it is*

I tell you. Bend down here today and look
at this strange harp, this
jeweled and busy zither, dead
and alive at the same time.

Here god is.

Laura Kasischke

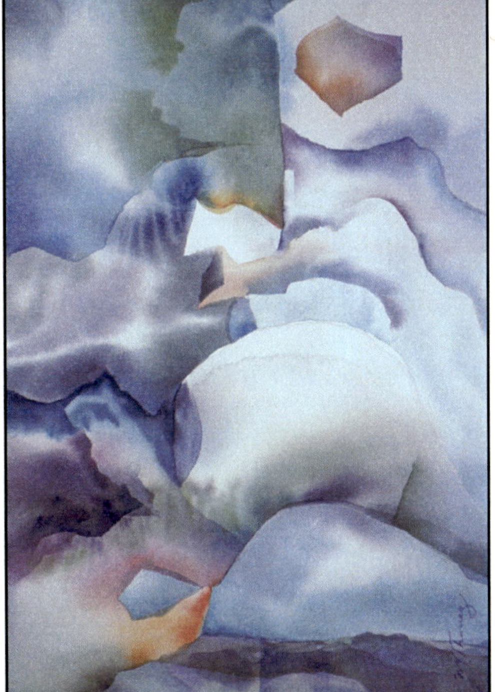

Whispered Secrets, *Monette Thorrez*

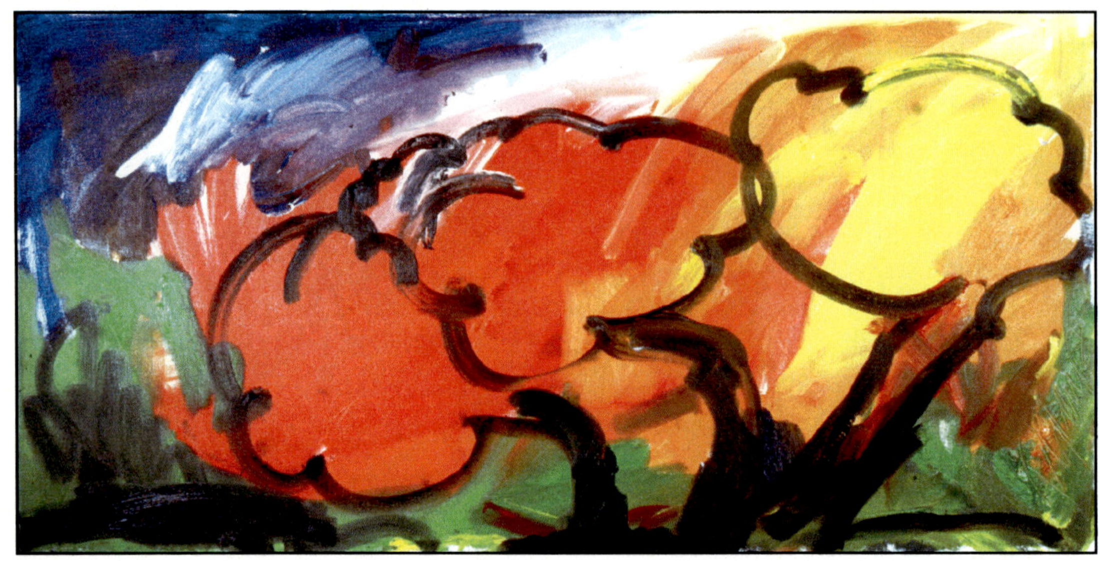

Into the Light, *Ruth Gilmore Langs*

Drought

There was no breeze today
I went through the motions—mine the *only* movement—
hanging clothes on the line.
It usually cheers me.

Yet today no flat objects sprang to life
as though their owner danced in air still...
Still, it was still. Still they dried
still they died, stiff, in rigor mortis, flat as road kill.

Now only carrion-preying clothespins remaining, perched
inanimately,
waiting...
the line is bare...my lines are bare.

No clothes, no breeze, no words, no dreams.
The child whose clothes brought life to my lines is gone.
They hang bare and parched
in drought time.

Hermione Miles Gorney

98

There Are No Poems Here

There is a mower, wet with rain
Against a stand of red cedar.

In the maple, a nuthatch
Walks up the tree and pokes suet.
I think it will be a long winter.

On the hill, the children
Yell and run and fall
Sounds echo from the willow

Which is here, as well
Raining yellow daggers
Across the green lawn.

David B. Sing

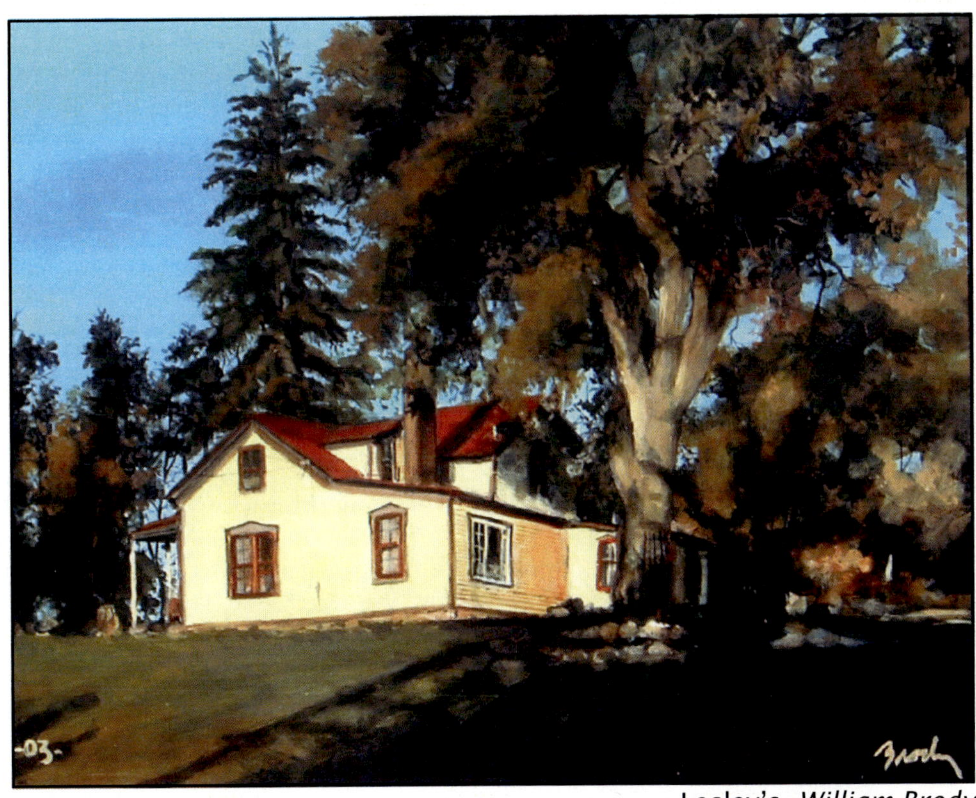

Lesley's, *William Brody*

Contributors

Poets

Rosemary Caruso: Chelsea Poetry Contest Award winner, Rosemary is an organic vegetable and herb gardener, who has a great love of singing, children, and elderly folks. She and her husband live in a cottage near a lake in southeastern Michigan.

Hermione Miles Gorney: Hermione grew up in rural Indiana, drawing strength from the natural world and from family stories of tough pioneers and immigrants. In 2003 she received the Harriet Storolow Creative Writing and Excellance in Education Award and won a scholarship to the Detroit Women Writer's Conf.

Marijo Grogan: Current Magazine and Chelsea Poetry Contest award winner, Marijo has been published in *Sojourners, Encompass*, and *Perspective*. Her award winning short play, *Star Wish*, was produced at the Heartlande Festival.

Carol Rose Kahn: Carol works as a nurse with the Washtenaw County Public Health Department, specializing on the rapidly expanding Latino population. Her dream is to one day write of her experiences as a nurse and visit Central America.

Laura Kasischke: Laura is the author of six poetry collections and three critically acclaimed novels. She has been the recipient of a grant from the National Endowment for the Arts, the Alice Fay Dicastagnola Award, the Bobst Award for Emerging Writers, the University of Michigan Hopwood Award and the Pushcart Prize. Her newest book of poetry, *Gardening in the Dark*, was published in 2004.

Judith Kerman: Judith is editor/publisher of Mayapple Press. A new collection of her poems, *Galvanic Response*, was published by March Street Press in 2005. Among her books or chapbooks of poetry is the bilingual collection, *Plane Surfaces/Plano de Incidencia* (Santo Domingo: CCLEH, 2002) and a book of translations, *A Woman in Her Garden: Selected Poems of Dulce Maria Loynaz* (White Pine Press, 2002).

Thomas Lynch: Thomas is the author of three collections of poetry, including *Still Life in Milford*, and two books of essays, *Bodies in Motion* and *The Undertaking: Life Studies from the Dismal Trade*, which won the American Book Award and was a finalist for the National Book Award. His newest book, *Booking Passage: We Irish and American*, was published in 2005.

Oscar Marx: Oscar is an award winning poet who lives in Chelsea, Michigan. Oscar can remember when harvest time was signified by trails of grain spilling from wagons as they rolled down the road.

Gregory Parker: Gregory lives in Grass Lake, Michigan with his wife, Connie. He is the 2000 First Place Award Winner in the annual Chelsea Poetry Contest and a Univ. of Michigan Hopwood Award recipient.

Susan e. Pulju: Susan won Third Place in the first annual Chelsea Poetry Contest in 2000 and her work has appeared in a literary anthology published by Washtenaw Community College.

David Sing: David is a long time writer of poetry who has among his credits editing and publishing several poetry collections.

Doug Smith, Editor: Doug is a past award winner of the Current Magazine and Chelsea Poetry Contests and has been writing and publishing his poetry for over twenty years. He is currently finishing up work on a novel about Detroit and hopes to have a collection of his own poetry published soon.

Jay Stielstra: Jay is a well known folk singer, peace and environmental activist, and the author of several musical plays, including *The North Country Operas, Tittabawassee Jane, Old Man in Love*, as well as countless songs.

Keith Taylor: Keith's work has appeared in many literary journals and several books. Two new books will appear in 2006: poems and stories, *Guilty at the Rapture* and translations from modern Greek, *Battered Guitars: The Poetry and Prose of Kostas Karyotakis*. He teaches part time at the Univ. of Michigan.

Richard Tillinghast: Richard is the author of six collections of poetry, including *Today in the Care Trieste* and *Six Mile Mountain*. Until recently, he headed the Master of Fine Arts Program at the Univ. of Michigan.

Brad Tompkins: Brad is a poet, writer, and teacher whose poetry has received recognition in the

Chelsea Poetry Contest and appeared in Washtenaw Community College's *The Huron River Review*.

Catherine Croisant Varner: Catherine is an award winning poet who has captivated audiences at readings with her dramatic oratory. She once gave a particularly stirring reading of Pablo Neruda's poetry at the Chelsea Little Professor Book Store for which the owner is eternally grateful.

Melody Vassoff, Editor: Melody is an award winning poet whose writing has been featured in several poetry anthologies and is currently working on a collection of her own poetry. Melody has worked as a bookseller for several years and is currently working at being a literary translator.

Kent Ashton Walton: Kent taught philosophy in London before moving to the United States where he obtained a PhD in Psychology. He has worked as a journalist and is currently writing a handbook on Nihilism.

Elizabeth Westrate: Elizabeth currently works as a Civil Engineer in Holland, Michigan. She started writing poetry in college and still tries to write in her spare time. She is working on an MFA degree in writing from Vermont College.

Sandra Xenakis: Sandra is a marketing coach, jewelry designer, and former journalist. Today most of her writing takes the form of advocacy for world peace. She is the 2002 First Place winner in the Chelsea Poetry Contest.

Artists

Ilona Brustad: Ilona has participated in several important juried shows such as the Birmingham-Bloomfield Art Association's Annual Painting Competition, the Jackson Area Annual Fine Arts Competition and the Ann Arbor Art Center's Annual All Media Fine Arts Competition, for which she has received several prizes. She regularly exhibits at Chelsea Painters Art Fair in Chelsea, Michigan.

William Brody: William has exhibited in galleries and museums across the country and Asia. Along with four one man shows, he has shown his work in such places as The National Arts Club in New York City and the Palm Springs Desert Museum in Palm Springs, California. He has won several national awards and is a Signature Member of the National Oil and Acrylic Painters' Society.

Mildred Dowling Clark: Mildred collected and preserved many photographs of farm life during her long stay on this earth, 1914-2004. She was the product of her times and would be very pleased to know that her photography appears along side the poetry of her granddaughter, Melody Vassoff.

Nancy Feldkamp: Nancy has won many awards and has membership in Michigan Water Color Society, Ann Arbor Women Artists and Pennsylvania Watercolor Society where she is a signature member. Her work is in the Chelsea Gallery and the River Street Gallery in Manistee, Michigan.

Alyce Frank: Alyce's body of work now numbers eight hundred paintings. Her work has been shown in numerous galleries and museum exhibitions and she has collectors all over the country and in Europe, Australia and New Zealand. In 1997 Alyce was the Alumni Artist at the Smart Museum, University of Chicago. She is represented at the Fenix Gallery in Taos, New Mexico, the Meyer-Munson Gallery in Santa Fe, New Mexico, and at the New Mexico Marin-Price Gallery in Chevy Chase, Maryland.

Teresa Freed: Teresa is an award-winning pastel artist whose work has appeared in many group and solo exhibitions. She exhibits regularly at the Chelsea Gallery, the River Street Gallery in Manistee, and at the Chelsea Painters Art Fair. She is a member of the Ann Arbor Women Artists and the Chelsea Painters.

Joan Painter Jones: Joan's art has won many awards over the years, such as the Hope College Award, Honorable Mention Awards at the Scarab Club Silver Medal Exhibition in Detroit, as well as a purchase prize from Del Mar College in Corpus Christi, Texas. Collections of her work can be found at the University of Michigan Hospital, the Jesse Besser Museum, and Saginaw Valley State Univ.

Sandy Knapp: Sandy is an award winning experimental artist in fluid acrylics and beeswax, and has been painting for thirty years. She is President of the Chelsea Painters and member of the Ann Arbor Women Artists, Society of Layerists of Multi-Media and the International Society of Experimental Artists. Her work is exhibited at the Chelsea Gallery and the River Street Gallery in Manistee, Michigan.

Mary Beth Koeze: Mary Beth's work has been in National Juried shows all over the country and had a one woman show at the Muskegon Museum of Art. In 2000 she won the Gold Award at the Great Lakes

Pastel Society in Grand Rapids and in 2001 won the Bronze Award at the Ella Sharp Museum. She is represented at the River Gallery in Chelsea and the Water Street Gallery in Saugatuck, Michigan

Heidi Kraepel: Heidi studied art at the University of Michigan, Wayne State University, and at the Univ. of Oregon. Her paintings are on exhibit at The West of the Moon Cooperative Gallery in Chelsea, Michigan. Heidi feels that fixing the world is an inside job. Making art is her own personal inside job.

Ruth Gilmore Langs: Ruth is an award winning abstract expressionist painter who has been painting for thirty years. Her large canvases embody the spirit of nature and create new ways to see the beauty of nature around us.

Katherine Larson: Katherine is a muralist, children's book illustrator and a classical singer. She is the owner of Diva Designs, a design firm in Brighton, Michigan. Her art has appeared on the cover of the Ann Arbor Observer.

Jean Lau: Jean has been an artist for over forty years. Recently Ms. Lau received a Best of Show 2004 award from the Ann Arbor Women Artists Library Show. Her work has also recently appeared in national and international collections on display in Ohio and New York.

Russ Marshall: Russ has been creating and exhibiting his artwork since 1985 at such galleries as Artsource in Flint, Focus Gallery in Detroit, Henry Ford Community College in Dearborn, and River Gallery in Chelsea. His work has been featured in Amerika Illustrated, Japan Time Magazine, New York Times, Mother Jones and the Detroit Institute of Arts.

James Peery: James has been a professional artist since 1990. He has participated in numerous one man shows and group shows. His paintings are held in private collections throughout the country.

Jacqueline Hoats Shields: Jacqueline received her Bachelor of Fine Arts magna cum laude from the Univ. of Michigan School of Art. Jackie grew up in Holland, Michigan and she now lives in Detroit with her husband, Gary Shields, and their two young daughters. She enjoys drawing and painting whenever she can.

Greg Sobran: Greg is an award winning artist whose worked has appeared on the cover of the *Ann Arbor Observer* as well as in several Michigan galleries.

Laura Strowe: Laura is an artist well-known in the Ann Arbor area for her etchings and pastels of local scenes. She has done many covers for the *Ann Arbor Observer* and participated in the Ann Arbor Street Art Fair for twenty-two years. In 2004 she received the Ann Arbor News Readers' Choice Award as Best Local Visual Artist.

Monette Thorrez: Monette lives in the country with her husband and two dogs. She is a member of the Ann Arbor Women Artists, the Cheslea Painters, and the Jackson Civic Art Association. Her semi-abstract watercolors are represented by Blue Hour Art Gallery in Marshall, Michigan.

Alexandra Tinsley: Alexandra grew up taking pictures in Chelsea, Michigan, and is now a photography student at the Pacific Northwest College of Art in Portland, Oregon.

Madeleine Vallier: Madeleine is a member of the Michigan Water Color Society, the Ann Arbor Women Painters, the Chelsea Painters and has served on the Board of the Chelsea Center for the Development of the Arts. She has had one person shows at the Michigan League Gallery, University of Michigan Hospital, the Scarab Club Annual Water Color Exhibit and at the Lansing Gallery

Elaine Wilson: Elaine received her MFA from Yale School of Art in 1983 and currently teaches drawing and painting full time at Washtenaw Community College. She is the 1996 recipient of a National Endowment for the Arts Regional Visual Artists Fellowship, and has had solo exhibitions at Sonia Zaks Gallery in Chicago, Bromfield Gallery in Boston and at the Alexa Lee Gallery and Tabor Hill Gallery in Ann Arbor, Michigan.

Karen Woollams, Editor: Karen designed and laid out the book. She is largely a self-taught graphic artist who enjoys creating and designing newsletters, flyers, websites, and an occasional book. She lives in and loves the Chelsea countryside with her family, including husband and fellow editor, Doug Smith.

Stan Woollams: Stan has been taking pictures for 50 years and plans to continue his quest for capturing the beautiful moment.